will encompass the whole gamut of lif
old age. Leisure without education
ful if we dare to increase leisure
reached until we have achieved a t
tion for the whole mass of the popu   ...s applies
as well to the leisure time of our 1   .y increasing aged
population.

An educated citizenry would laugh out of court a high
percentage of our current advertising—a form of "inverted
education." We are expending an immense effort to make
people believe things that are not so. This way leads to a
deteriorating society. Apart from the all-important problem
of national security, the issue that overrides all others relates
to social values. Can we muster that quality of leadership
without which the people perish? The sixties will unavoid-
ably become a battleground between the forces tending to
produce a gadget society and those pointing the way to a
truly civilized community.

The greater part of this book consists of six lectures delivered at Haverford College, where I served as Phillips
Lecturer in the autumn of 1959, and three lectures at Smith
College, where I served as the William Allan Neilson Professor in the spring of 1960. I am indebted to the departments
of economics at both these institutions and to the stimulating
audiences that attended these lectures. I especially wish to
express my thanks to President Hugh Borton of Haverford
and to President Thomas C. Mendenhall of Smith College.

Above all I am indebted once again to that amazing producer of highly useful books and pamphlets dealing cou-
rageously and competently with so many of the vital economic problems of our times, Professor Seymour E. Harris.
In his incredibly busy life he still finds time to read manu-
scripts for *The Economics Handbook Series* and to make
detailed criticisms and suggestions.

Finally, I am grateful to W. W. Norton & Company, Inc., the Committee for Economic Development, and the *Review of Economics and Statistics* for permission to reprint some previously published materials.

Alvin H. Hansen

EDITOR'S INTRODUCTION

For years many teachers of economics and other professional economists have felt the need of a series of books on economic subjects which is not filled by the usual textbook or by the highly technical treatise.

This present series, published under the general title, *The Economics Handbook Series,* was planned with these needs in mind. Designed first of all for students, the volumes are useful in the ever-growing field of adult education; they also are of interest to the informed general reader.

The volumes are not long. They give the essentials of the subject matter within the limits of a few hundred pages; they present a distillate of accepted theory and practice, without the detailed approach of the technical treatise. Each volume is a unit, standing on its own.

The authors are scholars, each writing on an economic subject on which he is an authority. In this series the author's first task is not to make important contributions to knowledge —although many of them do—but so to present his subject matter that his work as a scholar will carry its maximum influence outside as well as inside the classroom. The time has come to redress the balance between the energies spent on the creation of new ideas and on their dissemination. Economic ideas are unproductive if they do not spread beyond the world of scholars. Popularizers without technical competence, unqualified textbook writers, and sometimes even charlatans control too large a part of the market for economic ideas.

In the classroom *The Economics Handbook Series* will serve, it is hoped, as brief surveys in one-semester courses, as supplementary reading in introductory courses and in other courses in which the subject is related.

The editor welcomes Professor Hansen's fourth contribution to *The Economics Handbook Series*. It is not necessary to go over his illustrious career as a teacher, writer, and adviser to the government. He has made his mark on economics and public policy through his own work and that of his students.

In the current volume Professor Hansen deals with the great issues of the 1950s in their context of the coming decade. The book not only reflects his usual analytical ability, mature judgment, and forthrightness, but includes many original ideas. Inflation; growth and economic development; monetary and fiscal policy; the spending pattern of the American people; the current state of the theory of the trade cycle and its control—on all these issues and others Professor Hansen continues to throw a penetrating light. Here he also presents a vivid description of the economic state of India, where he spent the academic year 1958–1959 as the first Yale-Ford Professor in India.

Seymour E. Harris

CONTENTS

PART II. GROWTH, AUTOMATION, AND
THE DUAL ECONOMY

PART III. DEVELOPED AND UNDERDEVELOPED
COUNTRIES

APPENDIXES

PART I

The Inflation Debate

CHAPTER I

INTRODUCTION

This book is about the economic issues confronting the United States in the nineteen sixties. I do not disguise the fact that it is at many points controversial. If this were not true, the reader would not need to bother. But anyone who writes on economic issues may as well admit at once that in the field of political economy truth is not a little elusive. There is no Mount Sinai to which one may go to secure once and for all the tablets upon which the final words are written. The reader may often disagree with what I say, and he can quite possibly be right.

The world moves on, and the process of social adjustment lags behind. The New Deal was not ahead of its time; it was long overdue. And in recent years we have been consolidating and validating our gains, as witness the *Economic Report of the President* of January, 1960. But problems are again piling up, and I have the feeling that they are more difficult—technically more difficult—than those of a generation ago. And possibly also the task of leadership encounters greater resistance now than then. We still have with us, in no small measure, dogma and tradition. And so we are stuck at dead center. Not a few of our political leaders appear to pride themselves on sitting in the middle of the road.

We have indeed conquered mass unemployment. But unemployment is still a serious problem. It averaged 5.1 per cent

3

of the civilian labor force in the postwar period 1948 to 1959 (omitting the years of the Korean conflict). This means 3.5 million workers,[1] or nearly twice the aggregate labor force in the entire state of Massachusetts. It means a population (including dependents) of 8,750,000 without employment support. We complacently take this in our stride, and in fact there *is* no easy solution.

Paul Samuelson and Robert Solow have made the very interesting, though admittedly highly tentative, suggestion that it may require an unemployment rate of 5½ per cent to ensure price stability, while an unemployment rate of 4½ per cent might yield a price increase of 1½ per cent per year. Actually the figures for the entire period 1948 to 1959 are not far off from the Samuelson-Solow schedule, though not too much weight should be attached to these data. It may be doubted, however, that we can achieve both a satisfactory level of employment and price stability without major improvements in our anti-inflation weapons.

We are suffering from the serious delusion that there is a harmony of interest between the various goals we seek. We want growth and expansion, but we do not wish to be told that this tends to bring on inflationary pressures. We are charmed by the oft-repeated refrain that price stability will itself ensure sustained growth. Some of our liberal friends at the other extreme appear to have developed a pleasing modern version of Say's law, to wit, that "increased government expenditures will automatically provide their own tax revenues without any increase in tax rates." There is indeed (as also was true of Say's law) an element of truth in this. But unfortunately the hard facts of life are not quite that simple.

We have overcome major depressions, but the business cycle is still with us and it is throwing up difficult problems in

---

[1] Calculated in terms of the 1959 labor force. In addition there is an immense amount of involuntary part-time unemployment.

several directions both at home and abroad. We have achieved an unprecedented level of well-being for perhaps 80 per cent of our population in terms of material goods and private possessions, but we have scarcely begun to face up to the urgent community problems of urban living. And there is still an incredible gap between the incomes of the lowest 20 per cent and the rest of the population. Poverty has not yet been eradicated from our midst.

Confronted with a recovered Europe and convertible currencies, we now encounter stiff international competition in world markets. From here out we must worry not only about our internal domestic affairs; we must also face up to a troublesome balance-of-payments problem. This limits our freedom of action. We are again enmeshed in the international price and interest-rate structure. We no longer live in a sheltered world.

The problem of national defense (though it has an economic angle to it) I leave to those expert in such matters. I do not know whether we are still a first-rate power. But I *do* know that the subject is being debated by knowledgeable people. And that disturbs me. In the nineteenth century no one questioned that Great Britain was a first-rate power. National defense is indeed *the* supreme issue confronting us. On one matter at least there is no controversy among economists. No economist, to my knowledge, questions the economic capacity of the United States to provide adequate defense. There are no budget-balancing hurdles here, though at times high government officials, including President Eisenhower himself, have come dangerously near saying so.

Up to the First World War the gold standard and the balanced budget were sacrosanct. The gold standard is gone, but the balanced-budget dogma has enjoyed of late a considerable revival. And linked with it, as a substitute for the gold standard, is a newly born dogma—already a lusty infant—the dogma of price stability. This dogma has become in recent years a major weapon to beat down government expenditures.

Anyone unfamiliar with our monetary history might infer from current discussions that until recently the price level has normally been quite stable and that we are here up against a new problem. The opposite, however, is the case. Wholesale prices rose from an index of 100 in 1790, one year after George Washington took office, to 185 in 1814; fell from 185 to 75 in the next 30 years and rose to 220 in 1864; fell again to 75 in the next 32 years and rose to 250 in 1920; fell to 105 in 1932 and rose to 300 in 1960. The record is one of price upheavals, not price stability.

At the end of the nineteenth century prices stood (despite the violent fluctuations to which I have referred) at about the same level as six decades earlier. But the intermittent long periods of deflation were even more painful than the periods of inflation. In contrast, in the six decades of this century the long-run *trend* has been sharply upward.

The nineteenth century, after Napoleon, was for the most part a century of peace. The twentieth century, in contrast, has witnessed two dreadful world wars—wars that drained off from a quarter to nearly half of the productive power of the warring nations. Nothing more is needed than this to explain the fact that our century is indeed a century of inflation.

History reveals, as noted above, that except for very short periods there is no such thing as price stability. Confronted with these historical facts the ardent price stabilizer will usually reply that he does not really insist on rigid price stability but only upon "reasonable" price stability. Then arises the very ticklish question: What is "reasonable"? I have noted that in the current discussions even some of the most ardent zealots are, in the final analysis, willing to settle for price changes of, say, 1 or 1½ per cent per year as being reasonable. Two or 3 per cent, however, is usually regarded as intolerable,

One per cent or so is considered admissible, but of course not as an accepted or condoned policy. If, however, despite responsible fiscal and monetary management, the upward price trend should turn out to be 1 or 1½ per cent per year, this would be regarded as reasonable price stability. More than this would be thought to be creeping inflation.

Price stability is far from being a simple matter. *Over-all* price stability covers up divergent price trends within the price structure. Industries enjoying more-than-average increases in productivity should be able to reduce prices. Industries with less-than-average gains in productivity are compelled to raise prices. Painful price adjustments go on continually even though the general index of prices is stable.

And there are other complications. Should we stabilize the wholesale commodity price index or the consumer price index? The latter is heavily loaded with services. Services constitute one-third of the consumer price index, and this is in fact the area that has given us much the greater part of the recent inflation. The prices of services rose 47 per cent from 1948 to November, 1959, while the commodity component of the consumer index increased less than 14 per cent, exactly the same as the wholesale commodity index.

It is true that the recent consumer price increases represent in large measure a lagged adjustment to our new price plateau. The fact is that in relation to the price structure as of 1940, for example, services have not yet caught up with the general increases in consumer prices. But the more recent increases also reflect scarcities in the fields of medical care and low-cost and middle-income housing, and inefficiencies in urban transit services.

Over the long run the consumer price index can be expected to outrun the wholesale index because gains in productivity are difficult in the service area. Thus from 1913 to 1929 consumer prices increased 73 per cent, while wholesale prices increased only 37 per cent. Even though we achieve stability in the wholesale price index, we might still experience creeping inflation in the consumer price index.

One might argue that we ought to forget about the wholesale price index and concentrate attention on the consumer index. This would, however, I believe, be a great mistake. Wholesale prices are all-important from the standpoint of the manufacturer and the farmer. Over the long run we should have to expect a falling wholesale price index if consumer prices were stabilized. This would tend to put a squeeze on the employer. A falling wholesale price index is not likely to be compatible with growth and expansion.

Our examination of the current inflation debate will, I think, disclose the fact that we are not at all clear in our minds what it is we want to stabilize. And we are moreover not a little vague about what constitutes "reasonable price stability."

CHAPTER 2

INFLATION THEORIES
AND POSTWAR PRICES

The public debate on inflation has thrown up three leading explanations: (1) demand-pull, (2) wage-push, and (3) administered prices. I wish to examine each of these briefly, and I shall then apply the theoretical analysis to recent events. But first let me clear up one or two misconceptions.

Some Misconceptions

The wage-push argument is a tricky one, full of pitfalls. It is an undoubted fact that if wages were held rigidly constant, any inflationary gap would quickly vanish. Consumption would, under these circumstances, be held constant—indeed in real terms would decline. No society can for long experience inflation if it firmly holds the wage line. This much is certainly true.

One could say that the wage level (or rather the efficiency-wage[1] level) is the backbone of the price level. It is the pivot around which the price structure is built. Keynes put it suc-

---

[1] "Efficiency wages" means money wages corrected for productivity increases. Thus if money wages rose 10 per cent and man-hour productivity also rose 10 per cent, efficiency wages would remain constant.

cinctly as follows: "The general price level depends upon the level of wage rates and the scale of output." [2] And both wage rates and output are, as he explained, affected by changes in aggregate demand.

Now here is the tricky part of the wage-push argument. We are often told, even by responsible economists, that the mere fact that money wage rates, since the end of the Second World War, have risen more rapidly than man-hour productivity—this fact alone, it is said, proves conclusively that wages are the *cause* of the postwar inflation.

This may or may not be the case. The truth is simply this: No matter what the cause or causes may be, wage increases will regularly exceed productivity increases by the amount of the increase in the price level. The statistical relationship between these variables tells us absolutely nothing about causal relations. Correlations of statistical series only pose problems. So let us not be misled by the notion that wage increases in excess of productivity must have been the cause of price increases. It could quite well be the other way around: price and profit increases causing wage increases in excess of productivity gains.

The Demand-pull Theory

The demand-pull theory can conveniently be split into two parts: (1) the purely monetary theory and (2) the Keynesian or income-expenditure theory.

According to the pure monetary theory, inflation is due to a redundancy of money. At first thought this appears to be highly plausible, especially when applied to the immediate postwar years 1946–1947. But even here I am skeptical. Had

[2] J. M. Keynes, *General Theory of Employment, Interest and Money*, Harcourt, Brace, 1936, pp. 294–295; Alvin H. Hansen, *A Guide to Keynes*, McGraw-Hill, 1953, p. 185.

the ratio of money to Gross National Product (GNP) been no greater in 1946–1947 than, say, in the nineteen twenties, inflationary pressures would still have been very powerful. We have only to remember the postwar backlog of unfilled needs with respect not only to the empty family closets, the run-down inventory stocks of business, but also to the accumulated shortages of residential housing and of producers' plant and equipment. In view of these shortages, income and employment would have had to be seriously deflated to hold prices down. Within rather wide limits, the rate of spending under modern conditions can be high or low regardless of the money supply. I said "within rather wide limits." There *are* of course limits, both at the upper and the lower levels, beyond which the quantity of money begins to become increasingly effective.

The total money supply (demand deposits and currency) remained substantially stationary from the end of the war in 1945 until the Korean outbreak in 1950, despite the rapid increase in prices in 1946 and early 1947. From 1950 to 1955 the effective money supply (money corrected for output changes) decreased 6 per cent while prices increased 7 per cent. From 1955 to 1957 prices increased 7 per cent while the effective money supply decreased 3.5 per cent. Clearly the popular argument "more money chasing goods" does not explain any of the postwar inflations.

The role of the central bank, though of great significance, can easily be exaggerated. It can indeed in part determine one factor in the situation, namely, the quantity of money. But only in part. The money supply is in no small degree itself a function of demand. Expectations on the part of consumers and businessmen, and the expenditure decisions based on these expectations, may bring about profound changes not only in the rate of use of money but even in the quantity of money. Whether bank credit rises or falls depends in large measure upon whether businessmen and consumers want to borrow.

Often the central bank can do very little about it. It can of course control the volume of bank reserves. But the privilege which banks enjoy of borrowing from the Federal Reserve makes even this control elastic and stretchable. And even were this not so, the availability of loanable funds depends very much upon the liquidity of the entire community other than the commercial banks. In the United States this liquidity is so great that the commercial banks have at times loaned billions of dollars for business expansion even though member-bank reserves were rigorously restricted. They have done this by selling government securities to the nonbanking public.

The quantity of money can indeed more or less affect the rate of interest, and the rate of interest will play a certain role —in some sectors of the economy an important role. But expectations regarding the rate of return on investment are far more important than the loan rate of interest. Technology, growth of population, changes in consumer wants, government spending—all these are the highly important factors influencing the demand-pull.

You will see from what I have said that I am basically an adherent of the demand-pull theory, though not of the monetary version of that theory. I hold firmly to the view that there can be no sustained inflation without a demand-pull somewhere in the economy, though it may not be all-pervasive. Since 1948 we have had two exceptionally powerful demand-pulls: (1) the Korean conflict and (2) the investment boom of 1955–1957. These two demand-pulls lifted the otherwise flat wholesale price level to new plateaus from which it has not receded. Without these two strong demand-pulls, we should have had no significant increases in the wholesale price index during the last dozen years.

The Wage-push Analysis

A brief word about wage-push. Wage increases come easily in industries making rapid advances in productivity. But for the economy as a whole, the story does not end there. Industries capable of granting large wage increases exert an upward pressure on the entire wage structure. Low-productivity industries are therefore subjected to a wage-cost push. This is an old story. Cost-push has always been with us. It grows out of the differential rate of progress in different industries.

Administered Prices

"Administered prices" is a theory of more recent origin. Since the end of the Second World War the general buoyancy of demand has eased off on three occasions—1949, 1954, and 1958. In my judgment it is primarily at these recession points that administered prices enter the picture. In a large and possibly increasing area, prices no longer fluctuate from day to day in a flexible, competitive market. They are set by the dominant leaders; and competitors (if there are any) follow suit. In many industries three or four giant corporations control 80 to 90 per cent or more of the market. These firms set the prices. Examples are steel and automobiles. Price competition plays little or no role.

Administered price fixing operates nowadays in an atmosphere quite different from that of former times. We have learned through governmental policy—the built-in stabilizers and modern fiscal and monetary policy—to prevent any sharp falling off of aggregate demand in periods of recession. Accordingly those who administer prices are not under strong pressure to reduce prices. Again, leading corporations are nowadays quite aware that wage cuts cannot be made as they

formerly were in recession periods. Moreover, business over-
head nowadays is rapidly growing, partly due to automation
and the highly expensive equipment required to implement it,
and partly due to the ever-growing staff of technicians. All
this means heavy fixed costs, and this makes business wary of
price reductions. Thus from both the cost-push side and the
demand side there is every incentive to maintain prices in
periods of recession.

Five Postwar Periods: Wholesale Prices

With this obviously inadequate outline of theory behind us,
let us take a quick glance at the course of events. By breaking
up the postwar period (that is, the period following the Second
World War) into appropriate segments, the explanation of
price-level changes falls quite readily into a rational pattern.
First there was the inflation of 1946–1947. This was clearly a
postwar phenomenon similar to the postwar inflation of 1919–
1920. Here the basic cause is obvious. If you fight a total war,
you can expect inflation varying within limits with the method
of war financing. Secondly, there was the period from 1948 to
mid-1950—a period of 2½ years—in which prices trended
moderately downward. Thirdly, there was the Korean price
spurt. This was clearly the result of panic buying by both
consumers and business, induced by the shock of a quite un-
expected war. Under similar circumstances we could count
again upon a sharp price rise. Fourthly, from 1952 to 1955 inclusive we enjoyed price stability. Thus we arrive finally at
the somewhat startling conclusion that as far as *wholesale*
prices are concerned, nothing much needs explanation except
the price jump of 1955–1958.[3]

[3] The special case of the consumer price index will be considered in
a later section.

The Investment Spurt, 1955–1957

The years 1955–1957 do clearly present a special problem. Why this fairly sharp rise in wholesale prices? Was it a demand-pull, a cost-push, or an administered price increase? Was it the typical business-cycle boom with the usual upward pressure on prices, or was it a new phenomenon?

It was partly typical and partly different. It was definitely an unusually strong investment boom, particularly in producers' plant and equipment. Such booms cause price increases. In the nine cycles from 1894 to 1913 and from 1921 to 1929 the average increase in wholesale prices per year of expansion was 3.5 per cent. In the 1955–1957 boom the increase was slightly less—3.2 per cent per year. Yet there is no case in our history in which the increase in plant and equipment outlays from an exceptionally high base was so large as from 1954 to 1957. The *increase* in round numbers was 40 per cent. And already in 1954 these outlays were at a record high. In fact the 1954 outlays on plant and equipment were equal to the average for 1952 and 1953—previous high years. From this extraordinarily high base producers' investment shot up 39.3 per cent.

That this created a demand-pull in the heavy-goods area can, I believe, not be doubted. The price movements support this view. The prices of producers' finished goods and of producers' equipment rose 22 per cent from 1954 to 1957. The prices of metals and metal products rose 18.1 per cent and the prices of machinery and motive products 17.3 per cent, while factory building and construction costs rose 15 per cent.

In the inflationary sector of the economy (i.e., the heavy-goods sector) the wage-cost push theory does not appear to have played any role. While prices in the metals, machinery, and equipment sectors increased around a range of from 17 to

22 per cent, hourly earnings increased only 15 per cent. In the meantime costs had been pushed *down* by large productivity gains. Cost-push was no factor in this area. In the capital-goods sector the inflation was clearly a demand-pull inflation.

Over-all Inadequate Demand

In the economy as a whole there was no strong, over-all demand-pull. Aggregate over-all demand was quite inadequate to produce full employment or any reasonable approach to full utilization of capacity. The chart on page 11 of the *Economic Report of the President,* January, 1959, discloses increasing excess capacity—a widening gap between the production of manufactures and manufacturing capacity. Unemployment was running around 3 million and was in fact higher in 1957 than in 1955. Still, aggregate demand, while inadequate, was creeping upward. Expectations were moderately optimistic. Under these conditions the less progressive industries granted wage increases unjustified by the productivity increases in their own industries. Costs were pushed up, and prices were to some extent raised even though demand failed to mop up unused capacity. Thus some price rise occurred even in the noninflationary sectors, i.e., sectors other than the capital-goods industries. But these price increases were remarkably small. Omitting the producers' goods, metals, machinery, equipment, and construction, wholesale prices in the rest of the economy rose less than 3 per cent from 1955 to 1957. This contrasts sharply with the 20 per cent rise in the capital-goods sector.

Under these circumstances we encounter a paradox. Any effort to curtail over-all aggregate demand by monetary or fiscal policy, if successful, would only tend to push output in the economy as a whole back into a higher unit-cost area. This could lead to further price increases—smaller output, higher unit costs, and higher prices. It is therefore entirely possible, paradoxical though it may seem, that a restrictive monetary and fiscal policy *can*, under certain peculiar conditions such as those obtaining in 1955–1957, actually have a price-*raising* or inflationary effect.[4]

The Ratchet Effect, 1958

I am unable to see that administered prices played any significant role in the price increases of 1955–1957, but the story is quite different when it comes to 1958. Here the factor of administered prices did seem to play an important role in the prolongation of the price rise into 1958. Supported by the built-in stabilizers and the powerful resistance of trade-unions to wage cuts, the institution of administered prices operated to produce an increase in prices even in the period of recession. As Professor Galbraith has explained, the process of price adaptation is not automatic: it is the result of entrepreneurial decisions. During the boom years, profits may not have been fully maximized. The administered price mechanism tends to adapt itself somewhat slowly to rising demand, and it may continue to operate even when the increase in demand has abated. It is especially significant in this connection that as far as industrial prices are concerned, the price increases in 1958 occurred mainly in the equipment and durable-goods industries.

Thus the 1955–1958 episode was indeed not a case of the old over-all demand-pull followed later on by deflationary wage and price cutting. It was a demand-pull reinforced by the wage-push on the upswing, followed by a mild recession buoyed up by the built-in stabilizers and by increased Federal

[4] Cf. Charles L. Schultze, *Study Paper No. 1*, Joint Committee on Printing, 86th Cong., 1st Sess., September, 1959.

outlays—a recession in which it was possible for administered prices to hold the price line and even to increase it. Thus we got the "ratchet effect" in a rising price trend.

The Role of Farm Products and Foods

It is often said that in any of our postwar periods of fairly stable wholesale prices, such stability covers up a divergent movement of (1) industrial prices on the one side and (2) farm products and food prices on the other.

There is some truth in this, but the point can easily be carried too far. We are concerned primarily with the period 1948 to 1959. Let us first consider each group separately in relation to the general wholesale price index and then compare the movements of the two groups in relation to each other.

Industrial prices (i.e., all commodities other than farm products and foods) exhibit a movement broadly similar to that of the general index but with the following differences. The upswing movements of industrial prices are stronger and the resistance to declines is greater. Thus the industrial price index exhibits the ratchet effect to a greater degree than does the general wholesale index. After the Korean conflict spurt of 1951, industrial prices sagged only slightly and stood in the recession year 1954 only 1.2 per cent below the 1951 peak. The general index in the meantime had fallen 4 per cent. In the investment-boom spurt beginning in 1955, industrial prices had risen 12 per cent by 1959, while the general index rose only 8 per cent. Both indexes continued to creep up after the 1957 recession turning point, but the industrial index outran the general index by 1.1 per cent.

The net result of the stronger upswing push and the more resistant ratchet effect lifted the industrial index, by the end of 1959, 8 per cent above the general index. Thus while broadly speaking the movements were fundamentally similar, there did develop a spread of nearly 1 per cent per year between the two *trend* movements. This divergence *can* be explained by reference to the role of farm products and food prices.

An examination of the data will show that the prices of farm products and foods tend to fall fairly drastically in recession periods. Thus from 1948 to 1949 the prices of farm products and foods fell about 12 points compared with only 5 points on the general index. Again from 1951 to 1954 farm products and foods fell around 12 points while the general index fell only 4 points. In the recession downturn from 1957 to 1958, however, shortages of fresh vegetables and citrus fruits and reduced marketing of meat products drove prices up 5 percentage points. This was quite abnormal, and this unusual circumstance accounted in considerable measure (though not wholly) for the increase in the depression year 1958 of 1.5 per cent in the general index. But in the last half of 1958 and all through 1959 farm-product prices kept falling so that by the end of 1959 the index stood 15 per cent below the 1947–1949 base.

In 1951 farm-product prices and industrial prices were not far apart—both being around 115 (1947–1949 = 100). From 1951 on, however, they sharply parted company, as far as trend movements are concerned—farm products falling and industrial prices rising until by December, 1959, the former stood at 85.8 and the latter at 128.6 (with foods in between at 104.7).[5] Had it not been for the downward drag of farm products and foods, the general index would have stood about 8 per cent higher at the end of 1959 than it in fact did.

The net conclusion is as follows: The downward trend, since 1951, of farm-product prices has tilted the general wholesale index at a level about 8 per cent lower than it would otherwise have been. It still remains true, however, that the industrial commodity index behaved very much like the gen-

[5] The retail prices of foods stood, however, at 117.9.

eral index.[6] This conclusion is important. It shows that the industrial price index, no less than the general index, has been dominated by two principal demand-pulls: (1) the Korean spurt and (2) the investment boom of 1955–1957. These two demand pulls lifted the industrial price index to new plateaus from which it did not significantly recede. The general wholesale index, however, did recede 3 or 4 percentage points after the Korean spurt, owing to the downward pull of farm products. This still left it, however, on a new higher plateau, though not quite so high as the industrial index. Following the investment boom of 1955–1957, both the general index and the industrial price index have again settled on new plateaus, plateaus tilted slightly upward and with a moderate spread between them.

One supplementary comment—surely of the greatest interest—relates to the relative contribution of agriculture and industry to our rising living standards. The business community, particularly in the East, is sharply critical of the burden which the farm subsidy places upon the consumer. The fact is, however, that the trend of farm-product prices has been downward, while that of industrial prices has been upward—indeed to a point at which a spread of about 33 per cent has developed, farm-product prices being that much lower by the end of 1959.

This spread, to be sure, is narrowed when one takes account of the farm subsidy. Including the subsidy (indeed the entire expenditure on agriculture and agricultural resources of nearly $6 billion per year) the public still enjoyed as of 1959 a price differential (as far as wholesale prices are concerned) of around 15 or 20 per cent in favor of farm-product prices.

The wholesale prices of *processed foods*, though the differential is not so great as in the case of farm products, similarly present a favorable picture compared with industrial prices,

[6] This follows, of course, from the fact that nearly three-fourths of the general index is weighted by industrial commodities.

the spread being nearly 20 per cent. At the retail level, however, the story is different. At retail the price index for food stood at the end of 1959 at about the same level as the index for durables and nondurables combined. In between the farmer's dollar and the consumer's dollar are the costs of processing and marketing, and in between the food processor's dollar and the consumer's dollar is the cost of advertising, packaging, and distribution. While agriculture has made phenomenal strides in productivity, considerably exceeding those of industry, the service industries show little progress.

All this of course in no way condones mistakes made in our farm policy. It is my view that we should shift over from a price-support policy to a policy of income payments to farmers. The income-payments method has the great advantage that the consumer would enjoy low food prices and the cost of carrying unnecessary surpluses would be eliminated. Some surpluses we should retain. It is far better to have surpluses than scarcities. And it is far better to have some farm program than to have no program at all. Whatever else can be said of the farm program, there can be no doubt that it has had a stabilizing effect on the economy. Thus, for example, when the flood of agricultural products burst upon the world markets in January, 1948, there is no telling what this might have done to create a cumulating depression had it not been for the stabilizing effect of farm price supports.

CHAPTER 3

THE CONCERN ABOUT INFLATION AND SOME HISTORICAL COMPARISONS

Causes of Concern

The 1955–1958 episode has been seized upon to arouse concern about the inflation problem. The recession of 1958 did not quickly bring a cessation of price increases. Indeed consumer prices rose another 2.7 per cent from 1957 to 1958, and after a pause they continued to push up until November, 1959. And even wholesale prices rose 1.6 per cent from 1957 to 1959. The continued upward creep of prices became a cause of concern.

The worry is not so much about the relatively moderate price increases. The worry relates rather to what appears to be a brand-new fact in our economic life; namely, that while prices rise as formerly under the pressure of investment booms, they fail to come down in the recession period and indeed even keep rising, though at a declining rate.

The Nixon cabinet committee, on price stability and growth, made no secret of the fact that in periods of rapid expansion the upward pressure on the price level is always great. The committee also called attention to the virtual absence nowadays of periods of falling prices. But it did not argue, as some have, that this must be regarded as unfortunate. Instead it called the elimination of deflationary periods an important forward step. The committee noted, however, that if prices are not to fall in recession periods, they must be nipped in the bud in periods of expansion. This, however, is easier said than done, and at any rate it raises the very serious question whether really vigilant price policing would not also nip expansion in the bud.

Not only do people generally feel the pressure of rising costs on their own pocketbooks; they also feel it as citizens of their local communities. The cost of State and local government services did indeed for a while lag behind the general price rise, but in recent years it has been catching up and by now is putting a severe squeeze upon State and local finances. With a rapidly growing population and expanding community needs, even the traditional services of police protection, education, urban transportation, water supply, sanitation, etc., are hard pressed. Caught between the rising trend of State and local taxes, a rising consumer price index, and the urges created by ever more extravagant advertising, the average citizen has become inflation-conscious. This is true despite the fact that the purchasing power of his money income after taxes is higher than ever before in our history. The plain fact is that the general public *is* feeling the squeeze and is very much concerned about it.

Now this leads us straight to another important reason for the current concern. The inflation problem can be made, and is being made, into a powerful propaganda argument against increases in government expenditures, whether Federal, State, or local. We have always had with us very active propagandist groups who seek by all sorts of devices to convince the public that government means waste, that taxes are money down the drain. Community services for better urban living are apparently *not* to be counted as a part of the standard of living. Yet it must become clearer day by day to any reasonable observer of the American scene that the marginal tax dollar has currently a much higher social utility than the marginal pay-envelope dollar. The former goes into schools; the latter into tail fins.

Those who are against an expanding government role with respect to public services have found a highly convenient and, I fear, a powerful argument in the inflation issue. And it is being worked to the full.

1948–1960 versus 1897–1913

In order to appraise our great concern about inflation a bit more accurately, let us take a little closer look at two earlier periods in our history and compare these with our recent past. Excluding the immediate postwar inflation of 1946–1947, there remains the more or less normal period of the last dozen years, 1948 to 1959, though this includes the Korean conflict. The *only* earlier periods (and this is indeed a remarkable statement) more or less comparable in terms of fairly sustained peacetime prosperity in this century are: (1) the sixteen-year period from 1897 to 1913 and (2) the eight-year period from 1921 to 1929. This statement in itself discloses how turbulent our price history has been.

Consider first the period 1897 to 1913. From the standpoint of our problem it is a highly interesting period. It offers beyond question the clearest case on record of prolonged "creeping inflation" in peacetime. We have no adequate consumer index for this period, but the wholesale price index increased at the rate of 2.5 per cent per year compounded annually. The total increase in sixteen years was 50 per cent. The yearly rate of increase (2.5 per cent) was much too high according to the currently accepted criteria of what constitutes reasonable price stability. It was very definitely a period of high prosperity, rapid growth, and expansion. People complained, it is true, about the "high and rising cost of living." The word "inflation" was virtually unknown. Words, phrases, play a not inconsiderable role in popular psychology. You can't frighten people out of their boots with the phrase "high cost of living." The phrase may indeed be an unpleasant one, but it is not alarming or terrifying. The word "inflation," however, *is* just that. "Inflation" implies that something is about to blow up. And in fact, much of the current discussion partakes, I fear, of something unpleasantly akin to hysteria.

In the period 1897 to 1913 there can be no doubt that expectations about a continued upward trend in the price level *did* affect business judgments in some degree. Farm and real estate values were shifted to higher ground than current yields justified. Farm lands and rental properties were overcapitalized. The stock market gained considerable momentum, but there was no wild runaway market. There was no doubt some tendency to hold somewhat larger inventories in expectation of price increases. But creeping inflation did not develop into a trot. Runaway inflation of the German type has never occurred except in cases of wholly irresponsible financing and in the desperate conditions of the collapse of a defeated nation or one swept by revolution. These episodes mean absolutely nothing for us or for the solid democratic countries of Western Europe.

The plain fact is that the inflation of recent years, 1948 to 1959, has been much milder than that of 1897–1913. The upward trend from 1948 to December, 1959, was only $1\frac{1}{8}$ per cent compounded per year for wholesale prices and $1\frac{3}{4}$ per cent for consumer prices. Contrast this with the 2.5 per cent for 1897–1913. In short, we have actually achieved during the last dozen years a remarkable degree of price stability such as we have rarely experienced throughout our history. Indeed, except for the Korean spurt of 1951 and the investment boom of 1955–1957, the wholesale price index has been stable or slightly falling. The consumer index has been creeping up more persistently, but only at the rate of 1¾ per cent per annum—not a bad record when one remembers that this period includes the Korean conflict. Our record from 1948 on to the present is, I repeat, nearly twice as good as that of the grand old days prior to the First World War.

Nevertheless there may well be force to the argument that nowadays the public has become inflation-minded. Will not this state of affairs give rise to firm expectations about the future—expectations of a character quite different from those of 1897–1913?

As far as the general public is concerned, the studies made by the Consumer Research Center at the University of Michigan indicate that people who have lived through the sharp rise in prices from 1940 to 1960 are not in fact convinced that similar future price increases can be counted upon in making their financial plans. They are not prepared to risk purchases on the assumption that past increases can be projected into the future.[1] There could easily be a decline in 2 or 3 years. Who knows? And the stock market could fall drastically. Consumers do evidence some growing preference for stocks as against bonds, and the interest rate is rising, as was also the case from 1897 to 1913. But there is no evidence whatever of any hoarding of commodities or any widespread hedging against inflation, and there is no likelihood that any such thing will happen.

1948–1960 versus 1921–1929

So much for our first comparison. Contrast next the past decade with that of the twenties—usually rated as par excellence the decade of price stability.

[1] See Eva Mueller's article "Consumer Reactions to Inflation," *Quarterly Journal of Economics*, May, 1959.

Note, however, that while the *trend* in 1921–1929 was stable, prices were far from being stable from year to year. Wholesale prices rose 4 per cent from 1922 to 1923, and 5.5 per cent from 1924 to 1925. They fell 2.5 per cent from 1923 to 1924, and 4.6 per cent from 1926 to 1927. This is a far cry from year-to-year stability.

I should like to call attention to another matter, if I may be permitted a short detour—a point of quite unusual interest in view of the position taken today in banking circles. During the so-called "stable" twenties—stable as far as the whole decade was concerned—a strong effort was made by monetary reformers, led by Irving Fisher and John R. Commons, to obtain an amendment to the Federal Reserve Act making it mandatory upon the Federal Reserve System to stabilize the price level. The bill was, however, strongly opposed by the Federal Reserve Board itself and also by conservative banking and financial groups who argued that such a mandate would place the economy in a strait jacket and block economic growth. Today the arguments run quite the other way. Times have indeed changed! But I believe that the conservative opinion of a generation ago was the correct one.

The relatively stable price trend in 1921–1929 was in no small part made possible by the low level of farm-product prices, and this decline played havoc with agriculture. Overall price stability was purchased at a heavy cost. And from the standpoint of the soundness of the economy as a whole, it is indeed a paradox that this decade of unprecedented price stability—the decade of the twenties—was also the decade which witnessed the accumulation of more serious maladjustments than ever experienced before or since, maladjustments which culminated in the Great Depression of the thirties.

In contrast, the recent past, 1948 to 1959, presents on balance a more favorable picture. Maladjustments such as we experienced in the stable twenties have not piled up. We have had fuller and more stable employment than ever before in our history. We have had a higher and steadier rate of capital formation in relation to the Gross National Product than ever before. We have experienced a substantial, though I believe inadequate, rate of growth. We have accumulated over this period a far greater nest egg of savings per family than was accumulated in the twenties. The distribution of income has become substantially more favorable, though on this score we are again losing ground. The number of people who have suffered reverses, and there are of course such, as indeed must always be the case in a world of change, is relatively smaller than in the twenties. In the two minor recessions of the twenties, i.e., 1924 and 1927, personal incomes fell off fairly drastically with consequent hardships for the lower-income groups and for the farm population. We have had plenty of sweeping assertions about the evils of our current postwar inflation, but to my knowledge no one has been able to produce statistics to show any hardships comparable to those of past decades. One occasionally still hears about the time-honored plight of "widows and orphans," but this argument, thank heaven, has at long last lost most of its meaning. The last twelve years have clearly been better ones than the decade of the twenties.

At this point I would like to make another detour in order to stress a matter, the pros and cons of which deserve a little more balanced consideration than they have thus far received. It is the matter of the erosion of accumulated savings as a result of the postwar inflation. The rapid rise in prices in 1946–1947, after price controls had been removed, is of course the most impressive case in point. The consumer price index rose about 30 per cent in this two-year period. After taking account of the interest receipts, holders of war savings bonds found that they had lost about one-fifth of their purchasing power. There was, however, no widespread complaint about this at the time. I think it was more or less expected. It was regarded as part of the cost of the war. It represented in effect a substitute for wartime taxes. Had taxes in wartime been somewhat heavier, the immediate postwar inflation would have been less severe. The loss in the purchasing power of bonds was in effect a belated war tax.

But by 1948 the war experience had been fairly well liquidated. How about the erosion of savings since then? What would be the purchasing power in 1958 of a savings bond purchased in 1948? On the old basis (the interest rate has now been raised) the purchase price of $750 would have accumulated to $1,000 in ten years, a 33 per cent increase in nominal dollars. By 1958 the consumer price index had risen by 20 per cent above the 1948 level. Correcting for this price increase, the purchasing power of the savings bond would nevertheless have increased (not decreased) in this ten-year period of rising prices, by 10 per cent. The purchasing power of the $1,000 in 1958 was about 10 per cent greater than the purchasing power of the $750 purchase price in 1948. The accumulated savings did not melt away. The interest plowed back into the principle overbalanced the erosive effect of rising prices. As long as the rate of interest exceeds the rate of price inflation, the purchasing power of the accumulated savings will continue to rise, though less than hoped for.

Admittedly the holder of the savings bond, by plowing back his interest receipts year by year, had foregone any spendable income. The purchasing power of his accumulated savings had indeed increased, but in the meantime he had not been able to spend his interest income. It is, however, a fair assumption, I think, that small savers are primarily concerned about the accumulating principle, not the year-to-year spendable income that might be derived therefrom. It is at any rate of the greatest importance to note that the purchasing power of the accumulated savings has in fact, after the immediate postwar shakedown, been growing, not withering away.

The 1959 *Economic Report of the President* discloses the fact that in terms of *real purchasing* power the per capita savings deposits and savings shares of individuals have increased 55 per cent since 1948. This is in part due to the plowing back of interest but also in considerable measure to fresh savings in a period of high wages and full employment.

Suppose the postwar period had, instead, been one of considerable unemployment together with a decline in prices. A decline in prices means a dollar of increasing value. Would the purchasing power of the accumulated savings per family likely, under those circumstances, be higher or lower than they are today? Past experience would say lower. It takes relatively little unemployment to eat up all the family savings.

Surprise is often expressed that the Consumer Research Studies at the University of Michigan indicate that for the most part citizens still believe that the United States savings bond is a good investment even in a period of rising prices. The fact that the purchasing power of the ever-accumulating savings bond has in fact increased since 1948 is no doubt a part of the answer. Moreover let us not forget that even in a *rising* stock market, approximately one-third of the shares decline in value. The small saver can easily do far worse than to invest in United States savings bonds. Conceivably, however, some combination of savings bonds together with an investment in mutual funds might be a sensible program for the small saver.

The point I wish to stress, however, is the fact that alarmist talk about the erosion of family savings in America is just not true. The plain fact is that the purchasing power of accumulated personal savings was never so high as now.[2]

---

[2] The *purchasing power* (after correcting for increases in the consumer price index) of the *net* financial assets of individuals *per capita* increased nearly 100 per cent from 1948 to 1959. See the *Economic Report of the President*, January, 1960, p. 140.

CHAPTER 4

WHAT TO DO ABOUT INFLATION: SOME UNCONVENTIONAL SUGGESTIONS

I have been arguing, as the reader will have noted, that the twelve years from 1948 to 1959 inclusive have in fact been years of substantial price stability despite the Korean spurt and the investment boom of 1956–1957. Still the record could have been somewhat better, particularly if we could have avoided that last spurt. Our record in the past dozen years is in fact not a bad one, but I think we can do better both with respect to full employment and with respect to price stability.

Things Not to Do

There are some things we are now doing about inflation that we ought not to do. We should stop trying to scare the wits out of people about this inflation issue. Fortunately the public puts little stock in this alarmist talk about the "tinder of inflation lying all about us." If the public really did take these statements seriously, there could be unfortunate consequences. Our people, however, have a sound common sense about such matters. And while this hysteria probably doesn't do us much harm, let us hope that we shall have less of it in the future.

Another thing we should not do: We should not make the inflation issue primarily a matter for monetary policy. Excessive use of the monetary weapon would force us fairly rapidly into very high rates of interest. We should indeed repeal the arbitrary 4¼ per cent interest-rate ceiling. But we should pursue monetary, fiscal, and other policies designed to soften the upward pressure on interest rates.

We should not fasten upon the Federal Reserve System a mandate to maintain stable prices. It couldn't be done anyway. A mandate that could not be fulfilled could be very damaging to the Federal Reserve. Moreover the goals we seek are far too complex, and often conflicting, to permit such a mandate.

Another thing: We should stop being afraid to use specific and direct controls, namely real estate and consumer-credit controls. These controls strike precisely at the points where the battle is raging. They are not blunderbuss gunshots. Installment credit jumped 45 per cent from 1954 to 1957. These controls should be restored to our anti-inflation arsenal. The administration of these controls could doubtless be improved. For one thing, Professor Arthur Smithies has suggested that we regulate the lending authorities involved, in a manner analagous to the regulation of commercial banks.[1]

We should stop using the inflation scare as a political whip to keep much-needed governmental expenditures down. Government outlays should be decided on their own merits quite regardless of the inflation issue. And once decided upon, taxation should be adjusted to the budgetary requirements of a balanced economy. This may or may not be a balanced budget.

[1] Consideration should also be given to the control of financial intermediaries which play an important role not indeed in money *creation,* but in the *rate of use* of money (i.e., velocity). See Seymour E. Harris, *Analysis of Hearings before the Committee on Finance,* U.S. Senate, 86th Cong., 1st Sess., chap. 2, August, 1959.

Taxes are indeed the main bulwark against inflation. If we are to meet at all adequately our growing public needs, we shall, I believe, need higher tax rates. The 1954 tax rates are not sacrosanct, though both of our political parties seem so to regard them. We should moreover do a better job of tax collection. We should tap dividends and interest at the source, as we now do wages and salaries. We should tighten up on expense accounts and depletion allowances.

There is no platform that politicians would rather run on than one calling for a cut in taxes. But this is the last thing that any responsible statesman should advocate in a time of urgent public needs. Mind you, I do not mean that we should not have a flexible anticyclical tax policy. A crying need in this country, as our recent experience shows, is to place far less reliance upon a flexible interest-rate policy and more reliance upon a flexible tax policy. A reform urgently needed, which would add immeasurable strength to our built-in stabilizers, would be to "devise a politically acceptable means of automatically varying tax rates with the ups and down of economic activity." [2]

Automatic Tax-rate Adjustment

We should introduce an automatic or semiautomatic system of tax-rate adjustment in the first income tax bracket, so that the rate would rise and fall according to agreed-upon criteria of employment, degree of capacity utilization, industrial production, and rates of investment. Such first-bracket rate adjustments would in time come to be looked upon as just as natural and normal a procedure as the long-familiar interest-rate adjustment. As an accepted policy instrument, it should cause no surprise; indeed it should be expected. It should be-

[2] Arthur F. Burns, "Some Lessons of the Recent Recession," an address delivered at the Tenth Anniversary Meeting of the Joint Council on Economic Education, Washington, Nov. 19, 1958.

come routine procedure. Primary reliance should be placed upon this adjustment mechanism.

Tax-rate adjustment has a great advantage over monetary policy in the respect that it acts almost instantaneously, while monetary policy begins to become really effective only after the general liquidity of a rich community has to a considerable degree been exhausted. Tax-rate adjustments become quickly effective in view of our system of collection at the source.

Such a reform would be a long step forward. Not only would we have added a powerful anticyclical weapon to our arsenal; we should also be able, by relying less on the monetary weapon, to achieve a more stable and also a lower long-term rate of interest—a matter of no small importance for growth and progress.[3]

Countercyclical Accelerated Depreciation

Related to a flexible tax program is the matter of accelerated depreciation. This was introduced into our tax system in 1954. I heartily agree that accelerated depreciation is a powerful and highly desirable method of stimulating investment. But I deprecate the fact that we do not administer it in a countercyclical manner. The privilege of accelerated depreciation was one of many factors that caused the abnormal spurt of investment in 1955–1957—a rate of investment, as Chairman Martin of the Federal Reserve Board rightly said, that was not maintainable.[4]

[3] Merit rating, in State unemployment-insurance systems, has a perverse effect, since under this system tax rates decline in boom periods and rise in depression periods. Merit rating should be abolished.

[4] "An economy with a long-run upward growth trend of about 3 or 4 per cent per year cannot sustain for long an increase in business investment of about 10 per cent per year in real terms, such as we experienced in 1955–56." William McChesney Martin, Chairman, Board of Governors of the Federal Reserve System, *Federal Reserve Bulletin*, May, 1958.

If we really mean to do something about short-run price increases, we shall have to iron out the fluctuations in investment. This is crucial in any short-run anti-inflation program. A cyclically adjusted system of accelerated depreciation could do *something* to smooth out these extreme fluctuations. Such a program could take the milder form of deferment of depreciation allowances, or it could take the more drastic form of complete denial. Canada introduced the deferment plan in April, 1951, in an effort to check the Korean boom. The deferment was in effect for nearly two years. After the inflationary pressures had eased off, the deferment regulation was withdrawn. Thus an anticyclical policy was in fact pursued.[5]

In March, 1960, West Germany changed the depreciation allowances on producers' equipment. From 25 per cent of value in the first year, the rate was cut to 20 per cent. For subsequent years the rates were similarly reduced. Also the depreciation rates for houses were cut from 10 per cent in the first two years to 7½ per cent, and for subsequent years the rates were reduced.[6]

An Anti-inflationary Tax on Investment

And just as accelerated depreciation can be employed to stimulate investment when capital outlays are abnormally low, so a *tax* on investment could be employed to choke off such unhealthy and abnormal investment spurts as that of 1955–1957. In 1952 Sweden introduced a special tax on investment on industrial buildings, machinery, and equipment. The tax was employed during the years 1952–1953 as a means of checking an excessive burst of investment. In the recession of 1954 the tax was rescinded. But again at the beginning of the 1955–

[5] Cf. Richard Goode, "Special Tax Measures to Restrain Investment," *Staff Papers*, International Monetary Fund, February, 1957.
[6] *The New York Times*, March 10, 1960.

1957 investment boom a special tax of 12 per cent was imposed on industrial investment.

Contrast this anticyclical policy with anti-inflationary monetary policy. Anticyclical monetary policy has the serious disadvantage that sharp increases in the rate of interest profoundly affect capital values. In the nineteenth century that was not any serious matter. Property was not then held primarily in the form of securities. In the nineteenth century stiffer interest rates mainly affected the holding of stocks of commodities. Changes in the rate of interest thus had an immediate impact on commodity prices. And on the other hand, capital values were not seriously disturbed. Today the situation is quite different. It is simply obsolete thinking to argue that interest-rate policy can play the same role today that it did in the nineteenth century.

In contrast a cyclically adjusted tax on investment acts to deter abnormal spurts of investment without affecting the interest-rate structure and capital values. Moreover, small new and growing businesses can be exempted from the investment tax. In contrast, restrictive monetary policy tends in fact to discriminate against new business ventures.

Advertising and Inflationary Pressures

Countercyclical fluctuations in advertising outlays would clearly be desirable from the standpoint of business itself, and from the standpoint of the economy as a whole such countercyclical movements would contribute to stability. Unfortunately advertising expenditures tend to fluctuate *with* the cycle and thus serve to intensify instability and to add to the inflationary pressures in boom times. Consideration might be given to countercyclical adjustment of advertising as an allowable business expense in calculating income taxes.

The postal rates on advertising materials circulated through the mails could be sharply increased. This form of advertising appears to be an effective means of stimulating bizarre and wasteful types of expenditure. The great bulk of this material does indeed, it appears, go into the wastepaper basket. As such, it is a drag on the Post Office Department and must be regarded as a public nuisance. Nevertheless, it appears to be a highly profitable form of advertising, and this suggests that it does increase private expenditures and so adds to inflationary pressures in boom periods. It should be added that advertising over the telephone is equally objectionable and is indeed an invasion on privacy.

Pay TV and radio would make it possible to eliminate advertising altogether from television and radio broadcasting. This form of advertising is peculiarly obnoxious and is increasingly interfering with orderly programing. And there can be no doubt that it contributes not a little to inflationary pressures.

A general curtailment of aggregate advertising outlays would reduce private expenditures and so help to free resources for national security, for public investment in human and natural resource development, and for much-needed public services. Advertising, by creating inflationary pressures, prevents useful, even essential, public outlays.

The Government Role in Collective Bargaining

Finally, there is one obvious thing that can be done and should be done about the problems of the wage-push and of administered prices. The public should be represented at every important collective-bargaining table. Collective bargaining is indeed here to stay and we welcome it. Large business units are here to stay and we welcome them. American opinion has veered to the position, I think rightly, that big units contribute to efficiency. But is it not sheer madness to continue the obsolete fiction that the public has no stake in collective bargaining in a society so highly interdependent as ours? If no agreement can be reached, the government should recommend a settlement. The facts about wages, costs, and profits should be made public. No corporation should be allowed to raise prices for a period of, say, six months after the agreement has been put into effect.

Suggestions similar to those I have discussed have been cold-shouldered by both management and labor. This suggests a kind of arrogant disdain of the public interest which the American people will not long tolerate. Now that the government offers management and labor the protective canopy of full-employment policies, powerful trade-unions and giant corporations can scarcely claim the right to raise wages and prices in the dark. The public has a right to know the facts and to throw in its weight at the bargaining table.

What to Do with the Rising Cost of Services

The reforms I have been suggesting apply primarily to the wholesale price index. The consumer price index is something else again. It keeps creeping up, owing to the rising cost of services—transportation services, hospital and medical care, and house rent. Stabilizing the commodity index would not completely stop the rise in services. If we really mean to do something about this, drastic reforms in the fields of medical care, low-cost and middle-income housing, and urban transporation will have to be undertaken. We are reluctant to do these things. There are scarcities here to be overcome. But the answer will involve an enlarged role of government—a further extension of the welfare state.[7]

[7] The Forand bill, which received widespread support in Congress, provided hospital and medical service for the aged to be financed as a part of the social security program.

In April, 1957, the Canadian Parliament enacted the Dominion Pro-

The problem of inflation will require continuous study, and we shall learn by experience. We do not know what are the tolerable limits of creeping inflation. We do not know what constitutes reasonable price stability. We do not know how serious are the conflicts that will emerge in the pursuit of our various goods—the goals of stability, growth, and our international obligations. Compromises there will be. Price stability within viable limits will remain a matter of concern. The public will demand this of any administration in Washington. In this matter the American people and their government can, I believe, be depended upon to act in a reasonably responsible manner. The danger lies not in this direction. The danger lies rather in complacency. What is needed is not the banker mentality of caution, but rather the entrepreneurial spirit of adventure, of bold experimentation. I leave it to the reader to see if he can scan on the horizon that kind of leadership.

vincial Hospital Insurance and Diagnostic Services Act. Financed on a 50-50 basis jointly by the Dominion and the Provinces, the law provides hospital board and room, nursing services, diagnostic procedures, drugs, surgical supplies, operating room, anesthetic facilities, radiotherapy, and physiotherapy. See *Social Security Bulletin*, July, 1959.

PART II

Growth, Automation, and the Dual Economy

CHAPTER 5

GROWTH, PUBLIC INVESTMENT, AND THE RATE OF INTEREST

The Soviet Economic Challenge

In the United States the trend rate of growth of real income —that is, of Gross National Product at constant prices—compounded per annum, has been around 3 per cent during the last three decades. As nearly as one can learn from the most competent researches on Soviet rates of expansion, the Russian GNP growth rate in real terms has been around 7 per cent. The growth of industrial production, moreover, as distinct from the GNP, has apparently been considerably greater— around 10 per cent. In contrast, our industrial production, compounded annually, has grown only at the rate of $3\frac{1}{2}$ to 4 per cent, and our GNP, as I have said, at the rate of 3 per cent: in other words, about half that of the Russian rate.

If we could assume that these rates of growth will continue over the next two decades, the Soviets would catch up with us by 1980 at a GNP of $900 billion for each country in terms of 1960 prices.

It could with a good deal of justification be argued that the Soviet rate of growth is in large part due to the fact that they started from a low base. Possession of potentially rich resources, still largely underdeveloped, together with a physically strong and energetic labor force, contributed greatly to the possibilities of growth in the earlier stages of development. Moreover it was possible to import the whole accumulated technology of the Western world as rapidly as it could be installed, without having to wait for the slow and tedious processes of invention and experimentation. It can therefore be argued that once the Soviet economy has measuredly caught up, its rate of growth will slow down to that of the United States and other Western countries.

I believe that there is very much force to this argument. Nonetheless, it would be a mistake to become too easily convinced that the spread between their rate of growth and our own will completely disappear, automatically, in a sufficiently short time span to ensure the maintenance of American economic superiority.

There are certain factors favorable to growth which are not permitted to come into play in our system as we now operate it. Unless this is remedied, there is reason to believe that the Soviet rate of growth, while not so large as in recent decades, may continue to exceed that of the United States.

Basically the matter simmers down to this: under currently dominant political tenets, the Federal government is not permitted to play the role which is requisite for adequate growth.

A Reorientation of Thinking

The Soviet system presents a challenge which we cannot ignore. To meet this challenge we need a reorientation of thinking and policies. We are not doing so well as we should. It is my thesis, which I present for what it is worth, that a full partnership of private enterprise and government is necessary to provide the requisite rate of economic growth. If the potentialities of such a partnership are fully explored and utilized, we have every right to expect a higher rate of growth than we have experienced in the past.

It is a well-known fact that this partnership performed miracles of production during the Second World War. No one believed it possible until it actually happened. It is this kind of partnership which is needed in order to measure up to the production requirements imposed upon us by the cold war. It cannot be done by purely conventional methods.

Our current, easygoing business-as-usual philosophy is slowing up our pace. Our rate of growth was indeed 3.5 per cent per annum from 1948 to 1959, but this period included the Korean conflict, which stimulated the output of manufactures. From 1954 to 1959 it fell to 2¾ per cent.[1] We shall not attain our potentially realizable rates of growth unless the role of government is firmed up on more solid foundations than current policies permit.

It is sometimes argued that a partnership between government and private enterprise will finally destroy private enterprise. Experience gives no support to this fear. This partnership during the Second World War strengthened private enterprise. Our public investment in scientific research and in human resources, social security, unemployment insurance, government insurance and guarantee of home financing, rural electrification, minimum-wage legislation, etc.—all these have strengthened the private-enterprise system. Occupant ownership of homes, occupant ownership of farms, family accumulated savings, profits of corporations—all these demonstrate as conclusively as anything can be demonstrated in economics that the Dual Economy—the partnership of government and private enterprise—has invigorated private enterprise. The

[1] It should be noted that 1954 was a recession year. Accordingly the figure given above probably overstates the growth rate in recent peacetime years.

experience of Western Europe during the last quarter-century adds support to this thesis. Private enterprise operating in partnership with a welfare state was never so strong or so secure as it is today throughout the free world. As the British prime minister said after the recent election, the class war is over.

One could argue, as some have, that leisure may be as important as, or even more important than, growth. This could well be true at some future date, but in the kind of world in which we still live I am unable to follow this line of thinking. We shall need growth, partly because we have a long way to go before the income of the lower fifth of our population has truly reached the level of an affluent society, partly because of the large backlog of unsatisfied community needs, and partly because a peaceful world is not yet in sight.

Granting that growth is important, why is there reason to fear that our rate of growth may continue to fall below that of the Soviets, and what might we do about it?

First Things First

The Russians may succeed in maintaining a higher rate of growth because they are able to devote a larger proportion of their GNP to growth than is feasible in the United States under existing policies and practices. The possibility that we may be unable to match their rate of growth could in part be explained by the manner in which American consumer wants and consumer values are created by the powerful sway of modern advertising. A not inconsiderable part of our productive resources is wasted on artificially created wants. Machines with 300 horsepower, weighing two tons or more, are standard utility conveyance for one single person—the typical scene on any American highway. Involved is not only the waste of materials and productive manpower, but also the waste of a highly essential and limited energy resource. This is only one example of the waste we see all about us in this rich country of ours. Instead of durable and quality products that are prized more and more as the years go by, we deliberately create things that we soon tire of—things that an effervescent scheme of social values quickly renders obsolete. Never before has there been so great a waste of productive resources on things that have little or no inherent value.

The more pressure advertising is successful, the more will we reach a point at which private spending plus necessary outlays for defense will absorb so large a part of our GNP that little room is left for public investment in scientific research, in schools, hospitals, housing, urban redevelopment, resource development, etc. Indeed we have already reached this point. The Eisenhower Administration has been driving this clinching argument home day after day. Having reached this point, public investment becomes inflationary. Since the public is unwilling to pay higher taxes, it then becomes imperative for the government to hold public expenditures to a bare minimum in order to prevent inflation.

I suggest that this philosophy, if long pursued, will make us a second-rate country. I suggest that an optimum rate of growth cannot be reached without a change in social values which will permit a better use of our productive resources.

We need to reorient our thinking with respect to scientific research and education. We read in the *New York Times* reports[2] that the growing authority of Soviet science and technology accounts for ever-growing allocations of funds to these fields. Spending on science in 1960 was to total 33 billion rubles, an increase of 15 per cent over 1959. Four billion rubles will be spent to keep 700,000 gifted youngsters in boarding schools alone. The high priority given to education, to the training of scientists and technicians, has become common knowledge.

[2] October 28, 1959.

Public Investment and External Economies

Under currently accepted economic precepts, the development of power and other natural resources in our country is stopped at the point where the investment is self-liquidating. This is true whether the development is undertaken by the government, as in the case of the TVA, or by private enterprise.

Consider the TVA. It is generally held that no such project should be undertaken unless it can reasonably be expected to yield a monetary return sufficient to amortize the initial capital investment and to cover the market rate of interest over and above all operating expenses. Indeed the TVA has demonstrated thus far that it fully measures up to these rigid standards.

At the time of its inception, the TVA involved, it is true, a tremendous risk. No one knew whether or not it could pay out. Opponents regarded the whole project as a piece of political folly. And supporters were quite aware that they were assuming a grave calculated risk. There was, however, general agreement that if the venture could not, within a reasonable period, cover full amortization and interest charges over and above all operating expenses, the project would have to be deemed a failure.

Now the solid economic facts are quite otherwise. But this is a lesson that the country has not even begun to learn. Congress and the electorate have never grasped the fact that even though power and other resource developments may not directly pay out, they may nonetheless be economically profitable to the country as a whole.

To appraise the economic justification of any development project, account must be taken not only of its direct and immediate earning possibilities but also of its impact upon the agriculture and industry served by it. In short, account must be taken of the role of external economies. And while the theory of external economies has long since been fully developed, economists have done very little to educate the country generally on a matter which is of the utmost importance.

Yet the point can easily be made quite clear to the general electorate if one compares: (1) the profit outlook of a private corporation contemplating a power development in an area in which it owns no business whatever except the power project itself and (2) the profit outlook which confronts a private corporation that already owns all the industries in the region. In the latter case the increased profits accruing to these other industries by reason of the power development may far more than offset any losses sustained by the power company itself. Under these circumstances the private corporation owning all the industries would certainly undertake the power development even though the power project itself might operate at a loss.

This simple illustration explains precisely one reason why the Russian system may be capable of a more rapid rate of growth than the American system as now operated. Not until we are able as a nation to grasp the over-all vision of the impact of resource development on the economy *as a whole* will we be able to match, as far as this one important factor is concerned, the Russian rate of growth. To compete on equal terms, public investment in resource development will have to be pushed far wider and deeper than we have thus far been prepared to go. A case in point is the Canadian National Railway—a government enterprise. From its inception it was not a good paying proposition, but it played a tremendous role in the development of the country.

Obsolescence and Accelerated Depreciation

The Russian system may continue to provide a rate of growth in excess of that which we are able to achieve by reason of our conventional method of dealing with obsolescence.

Under a system of private enterprise, established businesses with heavy investment in plant and equipment are loath to scrap existing facilities and will certainly not do so merely because the new technology is more efficient than the old. New machinery will not be introduced, the old will not be scrapped, until it becomes quite clear that the new lower costs more than offset the losses involved in writing off the old equipment. There is, furthermore, the great risk that, in a rapidly changing world, investment made today in the most up-to-date equipment may tomorrow be rendered obsolete by still newer techniques. It may well be the part of wisdom to wait until time will have sharply reduced the write-off losses.

In the days of ruthless competition when new firms were constantly entering almost every field of manufacture, established companies were pretty much compelled to write off obsolete equipment whether they liked it or not. The new competitors entered the market with the most recent techniques. Old concerns were forced into line or driven to the wall. Survival required a rapid rate of obsolescence. Nowadays, when only a few giant firms occupy the field and when the capital required to compete runs into hundreds of millions and even billions of dollars, new entrants no longer threaten established firms. The firmly entrenched companies can calculate more coolly than formerly the cost of a write-off of old equipment against the economies of the new techniques. Pressure to introduce new processes is indeed strong, and vast sums are spent on technological research. But the pressure is less compelling in a monopolistic or quasi-monopolistic situation.

All studies, from Hoover's famous report on waste in industry in the early twenties to the present, disclose the fact that a large part of American industry falls far below the level of what could be achieved if full advantage were taken of known management and production techniques. Less than one-third of our plant and equipment is modern in the realistic sense of being new since 1950.[3] Under the Russian system, however, decisions to introduce all around the most up-to-date equipment can be made purely on the basis of productivity, not on the basis of profit calculations of giant concerns relatively free from severe competition or the profit calculations of smaller concerns in fields dominated by sluggish custom and practices. To be sure, Russian technology still falls far short of current technological knowledge. The available resources are limited. The GNP is still relatively small, and the amount of capital formation that can be squeezed out, over and above the military output and the urgently necessary consumers' goods, while relatively large, is absolutely small. Yet as GNP grows, the capacity to pump out capital formation will progressively increase. In the Russian system the speed with which obsolescent equipment is scrapped is not based on profit calculations. It is limited only by the rate of technical progress and the limits imposed by scarcity of resources.

An obvious solution or partial solution for American industry is to stimulate investment in the newest techniques by the device of accelerated depreciation. This amounts to an interest-free loan from the government to private business. Accelerated depreciation was indeed incorporated into our tax legislation in 1954. It should be carried much farther than the present law permits. But it should be administered counter-

[3] Dexter M. Keezer, *New Forces in American Business*, McGraw-Hill, 1959, p. 23.

cyclically. Long-term growth requires a rapid rate of depreciation and replacement of obsolete equipment, but stability requires a cyclical adjustment of the accelerated depreciation privilege. The burst of investment in the period 1955 to 1957 was primarily responsible for the recession of 1958. Bursts of investment are inimical not only to stability, but also to sustained rates of growth. Tax provisions relating to accelerated depreciation should be very generous in order to permit maximum growth. But they should be cyclically adjusted in order to foster stability and sustained growth.

Full Investment and the Rate of Interest

The Soviet system may be able to maintain a higher rate of growth than we can achieve under current policies because their system permits in the long run an over-all investment in industry as a whole to the point of "full investment." This means that investment in plant and equipment can be carried to the full limit of capital productivity, namely, the point at which any further investment (given the state of technology) would yield no additional net output. New techniques and a growth in the labor force would of course open up further outlets for investment. These new outlets could then again be exploited to the full.

It is, of course, evident that for a considerable time at least investment cannot be carried to the point of full investment in the Soviet Union. Up to date it has certainly not been carried that far by a wide margin. This is due partly to the fact that in the earlier stages of development Russia has experienced a marked shortage of capital goods. Thus the marginal product of capital has in fact been high—indeed much higher than in the more-developed countries of Europe and the United States. Moreover, even if the condition of severe capital shortage were overcome, it would still be true for a long time to come that the military requirements and the sorely needed minimum of consumers' goods would preclude a volume of capital formation large enough to reach the point of full investment.

But the outlets for investment in the Soviet system for the foreseeable future appear to be practically limitless. The outlet is large because Russia has still a considerable distance to go before her stock of capital will have caught up with the advanced countries. And taking a longer view of the matter, the outlets for investment can remain very large even after her greatly enlarged capital stock has driven the marginal productivity of capital down to the level of the Western countries. This is true because investment in Russia need not stop at the point where the net marginal yield will cover the interest cost. Investment can, if the party leaders so decide, be pushed on to the point of full investment.[4]

In the United States, however, operating under present procedures and practices, investment is stopped short of what it ought to be by reason of an unduly high rate of interest. In these circumstances investment cannot be pushed beyond the limits imposed by the prevailing interest rate.

Here again something could be done about it if we were prepared to throw overboard outmoded conventional ideas. What is needed is a sustained low rate of interest.

A low long-term interest rate is important for new and growing businesses. It is relatively unimportant for large and well-established industries. Businesses making large and stable profits are but little affected by the rate of interest, since interest charges are a cost of business and are deducted from

---

[4] Economists (Mises, Lange, F. M. Taylor, and others), seeking to apply the principles of marginalism, have sought to show that optimum use of resources requires that account be taken of the rate of interest not only in the allocation of capital to different industries but also in the allocation of productive resources to the output of capital goods in relation to the output of consumers' goods.

gross income in calculating the taxable corporate income. As long as corporate income taxes are 52 per cent, it follows that the government in effect pays half the interest cost of all corporations that make a net profit. Thus even a fairly high long-term rate of interest does not seriously affect large and well-established business. But in the case of new and growing businesses, profits are likely to be small or nonexistent, and so the full interest charge or nearly all must be carried by the business unit itself. To foster dynamic growth, we need new and growing businesses. They can be helped in the early stages of their development by low long-term rates of interest. Moreover State and local governments are highly dependent upon the bond market for flotations to finance projects of all kinds—schools, hospitals, roads, water supply, sewerage systems, etc. Inadequate provision for these things can seriously hamper growth. In another area—housing—the rate of interest is an important consideration. A low long-term rate of interest is therefore a matter of vital concern for growth and development.[5]

But are we not here confronted by a serious dilemma? How can we manage the public debt if we seek a low long-term rate of interest? In recent years the bond market for United States securities has become a cause of considerable concern. The Administration has asked Congress to remove the 4¼ per cent ceiling on five-year and longer-term bonds. Congress has denied this request. I myself would support the Administration's request. I believe that this ceiling should be removed.

[5] An example of the importance of low interest rates can be found in the case of the Dormitory Authority of New York State. The Authority builds and leases buildings to private colleges and universities. At 4 or 4½ per cent interest the costs are so high that the colleges cannot afford the rentals that must be charged. But if the credit of the State were placed behind the Authority, as is now proposed, the interest rate could be cut by perhaps 1 per cent, and this would make the charges tolerable.

The rate of interest should be controlled, not by fiat but by monetary and fiscal policy and by market forces. The ceiling should indeed be removed, but there should then be instituted policies designed to resist tendencies toward relatively high long-term rates of interest.

Inflation and the Rate of Interest

Deliberate use of the rate of interest as the primary instrument of price control should be abandoned. This policy is relatively ineffective as far as the large and firmly established corporations are concerned; and very often three or four large corporations dominate 80 to 90 per cent or more of the market. In the United States we have reached a condition of corporate financial self-sufficiency to a remarkable degree. The internal sources of funds—depreciation reserves and retained earnings—supply the great bulk of the capital needs. Thus large and highly profitable concerns are not heavily dependent upon bank loans. When, however, they do need external funds, they can usually borrow directly from insurance companies and savings banks. And if necessary they can often get bank loans, even in the face of central-bank restraint, since the commercial banks can sell their holdings of government securities to the nonbanking public—insurance companies, savings banks, building and loan associations, pension funds, etc.—and use the funds thus obtained for loans to business. In recent years the commercial banks have at times unloaded billions of dollars of government securities in order to increase their loans to business. And it is typically the well-established businesses that are able to get the loans.

The conclusion is that we can well afford to abandon the high-interest-rate method of controlling inflation. It is a relatively ineffective device. There are other ways to manage the problem.

A Low Long-term Rate of Interest

The long-term rate of interest is, to be sure, a market phenomenon, and I do not propose to fix it by act of Congress. In strongly expansionist periods the rate of interest will certainly trend upward, and there are limits, I believe, to how far this trend can wisely be resisted. But the market forces can nonetheless in considerable measure be controlled by deliberate policy. Some of the current market pressure which tends to push bond prices down could be removed by freezing a considerable part of the public debt into the portfolios of the commercial banks. This could be done by requiring, in addition to a cash reserve, a security reserve against deposits. This has often been proposed, but never acted upon by the Congress. This is the first step in my proposal to ease the pressure on the rate of interest.

Secondly, the Federal Reserve could play a much more vigorous role than it now does in support of the government-securities market.[6] It could do this without any inflationary consequences whatever. It could purchase United States securities, whether refunding or new issues, in the open market and offset the impact of such purchases upon member-bank reserve balances by raising the reserve requirements. The maximum legal reserve requirement should be raised. Better still there should be no legal limits at all, thereby leaving the actual reserve requirements completely up to the Federal Reserve Board. Any increases made by the Board from the present reserve rate would of course be made gradually and intermittently and might at times be reversed in response to the requirements of monetary equilibrium and changing conditions in the bond market. But in a rapidly expanding and

[6] See my criticism of the "bills only" doctrine in *The American Economy*, McGraw-Hill, 1957, chap. 4.

dynamic economy an upward pressure on the rate of interest can be expected, and therefore on balance Federal Reserve support of the government-securities market would be in order. In so far as the open-market purchases exceeded the requirements of monetary equilibrium, this would call for an offsetting restraining move by the Board of Governors (in order to prevent undue monetary expansion), namely raising the member-bank reserve requirements.

But this offsetting restraint would not always be necessary. A growing economy needs a growing monetary base and a growing money supply. Under these circumstances open-market purchases by the Federal Reserve need not always be offset by raising the reserve ratios.

It has been suggested that the appropriate method of achieving monetary expansion is to reduce the member-bank reserve requirements. This method is of course equally as effective as the method of open-market purchases. But there is this important difference. Reducing the reserve ratios has the effect of giving the member banks all the profits derived from the newly increased credit base. A reduction of the member-bank reserve requirements at once enables the commercial banks to convert an unearning asset (namely, the cash formerly on deposit with the Federal Reserve) into loans or investments. In contrast, the open-market method assures the Federal government of at least a part of the benefit accruing from the increase in the monetary base, since this method adds earning assets to the Federal Reserve banks, the profits of which, over and above expenses, flow to the United States Treasury. There still remains, however, a large profit advantage to the member banks. This is true because the newly created reserve balances (which accrue automatically to the member banks as a whole in consequence of the open-market purchases) enable the commercial banks to expand their loans and investments by a multiple of the increase in reserves—the value of the multiple depending upon the prevailing reserve ratios. Accordingly the banks can certainly not complain that they are being treated unfairly. The windfall is somewhat less but nonetheless substantial.[7]

This then is the second step in my proposal to ease the pressure on the rate of interest. It could do a good deal to promote a lower long-term rate of interest and so foster a more adequate rate of economic growth.

Obviously a program involving open-market purchases by the Federal Reserve, considerably in excess of the requirements of monetary growth, would tend eventually to produce the so-called "100 per cent Reserve" scheme. I have never been an advocate of this system, and I do not accept it either as a dogma or as a desirable system of banking. I should not want to eliminate the fractional reserve system whereby commercial banks can create credit whenever their reserve position permits such expansion. I should not wish to reduce commercial banking into a mere checking service institution. But I see no good reason why the reserve ratios might not appropriately be raised to 30, 40, or even 50 per cent.[8] This would reduce the

[7] On the other hand, it must be noted that when open-market purchases by the Federal Reserve have to be fully offset by raising the reserve requirements in order to maintain monetary stability, the earning power of the member banks is decreased. But in a growing economy the volume of member-bank reserve balances can be allowed to grow without raising reserve ratios, thereby increasing the lending power of commercial banks.

[8] Allan Sproul, formerly President of the New York Federal Reserve Bank, has said: "There may well be reasons, taking a long view, for an increase in the reserve requirements of the commercial banks. . . . [There may well be] a balance of advantage in higher reserve requirements, as a means of reducing the dangerous expansibility and at times, destructive contractibility of a money supply based on low reserve ratios. . . . [There may be] too great an element of leverage in our present system." *Hearings of the Senate Banking and Currency Committee*, 81st Cong., 1st Sess., May 11, 12, and 13, 1949, p. 69.

leverage in the banking system and would tend to strengthen the position of the monetary authorities. At the same time it would permit the expansion of commercial-bank credit in accordance with the requirements of a growing economy. The role of commercial banks as lenders of funds to businesses would remain intact.

Under my proposal the Federal Reserve would acquire an increasing proportion of the Federal debt. This would tend to promote stability in the government-securities market and would contribute substantially to effective debt management. The proposal is unconventional, but we do not live in a business-as-usual world.

Conclusion

I have suggested five specific lines of attack on the problem of growth: (1) foster a less wasteful use of our productive resources, (2) increase public investment in scientific research and education, (3) increase public investment in resource development, (4) accelerate depreciation to encourage private investment and hasten the scrapping of obsolete equipment, and (5) maintain a low long-term rate of interest to stimulate fuller utilization of technological developments and encourage new and growing industries.

CHAPTER 6

GROWTH,
PUBLIC CREDIT, AND TAXES

I have urged a far greater role of government. I have indicated
the need for a much larger volume of public investment.
Would not this run counter to a sound program of public-debt
management? Such a program might have to be financed in
part, at least, by borrowing. If this were done, instead of reducing the public debt, as is now widely advocated, would
not the public debt rise to still higher levels?

Debt in Relation to Income

Let it be noted first of all that everything in the field of
economics has to be viewed in terms of relatives, not in terms
of absolutes. It means nothing to recite, as some do, the fact
that the Federal debt in George Washington's time was inconsequential compared to the current $290 billion. What is far
more relevant is the fact that half of Washington's budget
was devoted to interest payments on the public debt. What has
real meaning is not the absolute size of the debt, but rather
the ratio of debt to the Gross National Product. In these
terms the *net* public debt has declined to less than half since
1946, i.e., from 125 per cent of GNP to only 60 per cent.[1]

[1] See the *Economic Report of the President,* January, 1960, p. 210.

Our GNP can be expected to rise by some $15 to $20 billion a year even though we achieve no great increases in the rate of growth. Thus a stationary public debt is in realistic terms a rapidly declining one: that is to say, declining in relation to GNP. And even though the public debt should rise by as much as $20 billion per year for twenty years, it would still be only 75 per cent of the GNP twenty years hence, far below the 1946 ratio. From the standpoint of ratio of debt to GNP there is no problem at all.

President Eisenhower noted in a recent press conference that the interest payment on the debt was now equal to the entire Federal budget prior to the Second World War. Yet the ratio of interest charges to GNP had fallen from 2.1 per cent in 1947 to 1.7 per cent by 1960. And it may also be noted, by way of historical comparison, that after the Civil War, interest charges were about double the aggregate Federal expenditures for all purposes prior to the war.[2]

The public debt, however, has to be judged on its own merits. Is it a good or a bad thing? Like almost everything else in economic life, it is both. Its size relative to national income is one thing to consider, and on this score I do not think we need worry. At the current ratio to GNP the benefits may well outweigh the disadvantages. What are some of the things we gain by having a fairly large public debt? They are very real, and we would miss them greatly if the debt by some magic suddenly disappeared. Emerson once said: "Be careful what you wish; it might be granted." And so it is in economics. Many of the things we complain about are things we would only learn to appreciate once they were gone.

[2] See Lewis H. Kimmel, *Federal Budget and Fiscal Policy, 1789–1958*, Brookings Institution, 1959, p. 106.

The Public Debt as Stabilizer

For one thing the public debt is one of our very important built-in stabilizers. This is peculiarly true for the United States by reason of the widespread popular ownership of government securities. This applies not only to the $50 billion of savings bonds so widely held throughout the country, but also to the $50 billion of government securities held in trust for the people by the savings banks, life insurance companies, State and local governments, savings and loan associations, and pension trust funds. Moreover, all depositors in commercial banks enjoy the security provided by nearly $95 billion of United States securities held by commercial banks and by the Federal Reserve banks. Finally $55 billion of government securities are held in trust under the social security program. Out of the total of $290 billion debt, $250 billion is in effect held in trust for pretty much the entire population. A part of this provides a purchasing power upon which to fall back in recession periods. And even though it is not drawn upon, it strengthens consumer confidence. This is one of the reasons why consumer expenditures have not declined, as in former times, in recent recession periods.

With respect to the great importance of a wide distribution in the holdings of the public debt, Abraham Lincoln put the matter in clear perspective. "Held, as it is, for the most part by our own people, it has become a substantial branch of the national, though private, property. For obvious reasons the more nearly this property can be distributed among all the people the better. . . . Men readily perceive that they cannot be much oppressed by a debt which they owe to themselves." [3] The debt could indeed be oppressive if it were held

[3] *Messages and Papers of the Presidents*, vol. 8, pp. 3448–3449, quoted in Lewis H. Kimmel, *op. cit.*, p. 65.

primarily by the very rich and if the tax structure were heavily regressive.

Private Debt and Public Debt

Another point of great importance is the well-known fact that when public debt increases, private debt tends to rise relatively little, or even to fall. It appears to be a fact that the ratio of aggregate debt (public and private) to GNP tends to be highly stable. Thus aggregate debt (public and private) was 183 per cent of GNP in 1929, 189 per cent in 1940, 190 per cent in 1946, and 173 per cent in 1959. Federal debt increased by $28.3 billion from 1929 to 1940 while private debt decreased by $32.6 billion. From 1946 to 1959 the net Federal debt[4] increased by $13.3 billion, while private debt increased by the enormous figure of $374.9 billion.

Now, which represents the greater burden on the economy as a whole—the interest charges on private debt or the taxes paid to cover charges on the public debt? The answer is certainly not obvious. It depends upon a great many factors. But one thing is clear. In a depression the tax liabilities sharply decline, easing the burden in this difficult period. On the other hand, interest charges on private debt remain fixed, depression or no depression. Again it is the built-in stabilizer feature of the public debt that weighs in the balance.

Public Debt and Monetary Liquidity

Consider also the impact of the public debt upon monetary liquidity. It is possible to have too much liquidity, and it is

[4] *Economic Report of the President*, January, 1960, p. 210. The net Federal debt here referred to must be distinguished from the gross public debt and guaranteed issues—the figure commonly cited. The net Federal debt eliminates certain types of duplicating governmental debt. See *Survey of Current Business*, October, 1950.

possible to have too little. It is my view, and it is shared by many economists, that in recent years we have had too little liquidity. A nation's liquidity in modern times consists of the money supply plus the outstanding public debt. Demand deposits, currency, and public debt—these together constitute our liquid assets. Now as a nation grows, it needs more liquid assets. It needs not only a larger money supply, but also a growth in the public debt more or less in proportion to the growth in the GNP. The money supply can be based either on private debt or on public debt, but it is in fact based on one or the other. Formerly the money supply was primarily based on private debt. Modern nations, however, have by now had long experience in developing efficient monetary systems built in large part on public debt. This process indeed began with the founding of the Bank of England in 1694. The note issues of the newly established bank were based on the public debt. And in our system today, our "high-powered" money—i.e., the note and deposit liabilities of the Federal Reserve banks—is based largely on United States securities. Moreover some $65 billion of the deposits of the commercial banks are backed on the asset side of the ledger by United States securities. And it is well to remember that the public debt plays a role not only in the creation of the money supply, but in addition it itself constitutes the major part of aggregate liquid assets.

There are good reasons for believing that a country like the United States with a GNP of $500 billion could not function effectively without a high degree of liquidity. As the GNP rises, long-run, restrictive tendencies could well develop by reason of an inadequate volume of liquid assets if in fact the public debt were not permitted to rise at all. And matters would be still worse if we should be foolish enough to undertake a drastic reduction of the public debt.

Restrictive Tendencies in the Late Fifties

Restrictive tendencies have already been at work since the end of the Korean conflict. The annual compound rate of increase of the GNP in real terms was 2¾ per cent from 1953 to 1955 and only 2.0 per cent from 1955 to 1959. We have been running far below capacity output. The chart on page 11 of the *Economic Report of the President*, January, 1959, discloses a rapidly growing gap between the production of manufactures and manufacturing capacity. Output has been lagging far behind capacity. We have been running (if I read the relevant data correctly) around an average of $30 billion per year below our GNP potential throughout the six-year period since 1953.[5] This represents a cumulative loss in these six years of around $180 billion dollars. In the last quarter of 1957 and the whole of 1958, the loss of output was exceptionally great. Professor Richard Ruggles of Yale has estimated that the rate of output at the bottom of the 1958 recession was $100 billion below the potentially possible rate. The average loss for the whole year was of course considerably less, but in September, 1959, he believed that we were still $50 billion below our GNP potential.[6] He suggests that the degree of capacity utilization nowadays involves not merely plant and equipment capacity, but also capacity in terms of the technicians employed. Automation demands technicians rather than operatives. Technicians are not discharged in recession periods. Thus with only a small increase in the employment of operatives, an enormous increase in output is

[5] Calculated on the basis of data contained in *Prices, Productivity, and Income*, Joint Committee on Printing, 85th Cong., 1st Sess., table 5, p. 91.

[6] See statement by Richard and Nancy Ruggles before the Joint Economic Committee, September 24, 1959.

possible by reason of the underutilization of fixed capital and of technicians. He believes that the potential increase in output is far greater than the unemployment figures would seem to show.

It is high time that we modernize our system of built-in stabilizers. Until we do this, we shall not escape the bugaboo of inflation every time we begin to approach full utilization. We need inflation-resisting cushions to make us bolder in our programs of expansion. We have been far too devoted to obsolete and conventional methods. As a result we were licked before we got started. On the basis of currently accepted practices, we cannot hope to achieve tolerably full utilization of productive capacity of equipment, technicians, and labor force.

Growth and Credit Expansion

In a growing society an expansion of credit, public and private, is not only permissible but necessary. In such a society investment must exceed saving. Credit must fill the gap. Up to a point, the government can legitimately finance through borrowing, especially in periods of recession, and a part of this may quite properly be taken up by the banking system. For the rest, the government can and must finance the larger part of its program of investment from additional taxes and by borrowing from the nonbanking public. How much should be financed from each of these sources must be determined on the basis of the requirements of a balanced economy. It is entirely possible that we shall not be able to achieve full capacity utilization of our productive resources in the United States under existing conditions unless we are prepared to tap by loan financing a part of the vast potential savings which full utilization would generate and in addition to finance by public borrowing some part of the excess of investment over saving which characterizes a growing economy. We forget that we have been engaged fairly heavily in loan financing in recent years, quite apart from the huge $13 billion deficit of fiscal 1959, which saved us from a really serious depression. It was only in the inflation years 1956 to 1957 that the budget was overbalanced. Note this point: In all the years of relative price stability, we ran a deficit—a deficit averaging $6 billion per year for the four price-stable years from 1952 to 1955 inclusive.[7] These deficits were not inflationary. They were expansionist, but they were not excessively expansionist. In much of this period we had far too much unused capacity. We were not achieving our output potential. We were not reaching adequate rates of growth. Public investment, especially in human resources, education, and the like, was altogether too low. Our budgets, far from being too large, have been too small—too small in terms of needs, too small in terms of growth, and too small in terms of pushing the economy toward full employment and the most economical utilization of capacity.

Growth and Taxes

I do not, however, wish to leave the impression that no sacrifices are necessary. Numerous forward-looking groups, including the Democratic Advisory Council (see statement of December 6, 1959), seem to argue that an expanding role of government, in the interest of adequate growth, will not necessitate any increase in taxation; indeed tax reduction is suggested on the theory that growth will provide adequate tax revenues even at reduced tax rates. This, I fear, is wishful thinking. If the Federal government is to play the expanded role commensurate with the needs of this critical period in our history

[7] The "cash budget" deficit was of course much less, but still it averaged $2.8 billion per year from 1952 to 1955 inclusive.

in terms of (1) defense, (2) growth, (3) foreign aid, and (4) the accumulating backlog of public service deficiencies— if these needs are to be met, I do not believe that fiscal responsibility will permit any tax reduction.[8] Indeed an increase in tax rates is more probable. It is true that part of the increased revenue needed can come from tax reform and from greater efficiency in tax collection; and it is possible that part of the increased expenditures can, as I have indicated above, be loan-financed. Nevertheless the job that lies ahead of us in the decade of the sixties is so great that a reorientation of our political thinking is urgently called for. Are we prepared to make sacrifices, or do we demand windfalls? As always, the answer runs largely in terms of the quality and character of our leadership.

There are too many variables to permit any dogmatic assertions with respect to the size of the budget or how it should be financed. The larger the government budgets, the more will it become necessary to offset the expansionist effect by surpluses. There are too many unknowns in the equation. There are no easy answers. Rigid formulas will not do. We shall be compelled to watch the economic thermometer day by day, as we undertake the risks of a great enterprise.

Caution, restraint, and complacency have been too long in the saddle. In our rapidly changing and challenging world we have been reluctant to try new approaches, to dare new policies; and we are loath to demand personal sacrifices. We are afraid of ourselves; we hesitate to use the vast powers of our own democratic government for growth and expansion.

---

[8] I repeat that this does not forbid a cyclically adjusted tax reduction in periods of recession.

CHAPTER 7

AUTOMATION
AND PYRAMID BUILDING

The historical process is a continuing movement, and for the most part, changes occur slowly and gradually, often almost unnoticed. Then all of a sudden there is a breakthrough, and one becomes aware that something important has happened. Though the term is often overworked, still it cannot be denied that there are turning points in history, sometimes well-defined and sometimes only broadly discernible.

An example of this process of change is the role of automation in the modern economy. Automation is a system of manufacture in which many or all of the processes are automatically performed or controlled.[1] The whole development of machinery, from the steam engine on, is more or less an application of the process of automation. Since the end of the Second World War, however, along with the increasing development of electronics, mechanization and automation have been growing with accelerated speed.

[1] Automation cannot easily be defined. One company has recorded over 40 definitions. The complaint is made that "it has no precise definition accepted by all." See "Automation and Recent Trends," *Hearings before the Subcommittee on Economic Stabilization of the Joint Economic Committee,* 85th Cong., 1st Sess., November, 1957.

Agricultural Employment

Take the case of agriculture. In Japan and China agriculture is still nearly 100 per cent performed by hand labor. In Western Europe and the United States, however, agriculture is today a highly mechanized industry. One man with machinery can now farm several hundred acres. The combined application of mechanics and chemistry has increased productivity per worker in agriculture in the last four decades considerably more than the gains we have witnessed in industry. Time was, even in this country, when 80 to 90 per cent of the population was engaged in agriculture. Now it is less than 8 per cent. And if the submarginal farmers were eliminated, it is estimated that only 4 per cent of the labor force would need to work in agriculture to feed, and feed well, the entire population of the United States—180 million persons. All this despite the fact that millions of acres have been taken out of farm use—indeed over 1 million acres are taken out of agriculture every year and turned into express highways and suburban development sites—residential and industrial.

All this means that we are approaching incredibly close to 100 per cent mechanization in agriculture. When you get down to as low a figure as 4 per cent, how much further can you go?

Now, as many people quite naturally ask, suppose this process also moves on toward 100 per cent automation and mechanization in manufacturing. What will then happen to employment? Will not all this vaunted prosperity lead to catastrophic unemployment, and so to a complete social revolution?

Employment Decline in Material-goods Sector

But first let us take a look at industry. How far has the process of automation and mechanization gone? Is it following hard upon agriculture? Is industry also moving relentlessly toward the well-nigh complete elimination of labor already witnessed in agriculture?

Here I have come upon what seemed to me, at any rate, a startling discovery. Let us divide our wage and salaried workers into two categories: (1) those engaged in the production of "material goods"—manufacturing, mining, agriculture, and construction—and (2) those engaged in the "service" industries—trade, finance, service activities of all kinds, government services (Federal, State, and local), transportation, and public utilities.

Now the striking thing is this: The material-goods sector was far and away ahead of the services sector in the early nineteen twenties—indeed some 10 million ahead in the number employed.[2] By 1940 material-goods employment was still well ahead—22.5 million employed against only 19 million in the service sector. From 1940 to 1947 (omitting the distorted war years) both sectors continued to grow more or less side by side, the material-goods sector gaining 4 million while the service sector gained 6 million. The material-goods sector was still ahead by 1.2 million as late as 1947. From 1947 on, however, their paths separated. After 1947 the material-goods sector ceased to grow so far as employment was concerned; output of course continued to expand. Technological progress and automation had put a ceiling on the number employed in the production of material goods. Indeed from 1947 to 1959[3]

[2] See Evan Claque, *Hearings of the Joint Economic Committee*, 86th Cong., 1st Sess., April 25, 27, and 28, 1959, p. 486.

[3] The last five years of this twelve-year period averaged exactly the same (26.1 million) as the first five years.

employment in this sector fell off by just 1 million workers. The service sector continued, however, to bounce forward with a gain of 7.1 million workers in the twelve-year period. And so by 1959 the race between the two sectors had gone overwhelmingly to the service sector: material-goods employment only 25.4 million, service 32.4 million.[4] From being 10 million ahead in the twenties, the material-goods sector by 1959 was trailing 7 million behind.

Thus the year 1947 marks a striking milestone in the changing structure of the labor force. Technology and automation have frozen the volume of employment in the material-goods sector—indeed have forced a decline. The service sector was absorbing the entire labor population growth. The relative output in the two areas is another matter, but in terms of employment a great shift percentagewise was under way—a shift away from material goods toward services. This fact, I think all must agree, is indicative of the profound impact of modern technology and automation upon the structure of our economy. It is a significant turning point in our history.

The cessation of growth of wage and salaried workers' employment in the material-goods sector from 1947 on is all the more remarkable when one keeps in mind two powerful new developments which one might have expected fully to offset the tendency which I have noted. I refer to the fact that the employment ceiling in the material-goods sector came in just the decade which witnessed (1) a tremendous upsurge in population growth and (2) a massive increase in expenditures on military hardware, induced by the Korean conflict[5] and later by the cold war. Both these offsetting factors might, one

[4] *Economic Report of the President*, January, 1959, pp. 158, 164.

[5] The trend after 1947 was at first pretty much a flat plateau, though the one year 1953 penetrated the plateau. This was due to a spurt of employment in the production of material goods induced by the Korean conflict build-up.

should have supposed, have caused a sufficient increase in the demand for material goods to sustain a rising employment trend in this area despite the spread of automation. That this did not happen underscores the unmistakable fact that something new has indeed happened in our economy. We have reached a sharp turning point in the relative employment opportunities of the material-goods sector as compared with the service sector.

So we get back to our problem: if automation is continually cutting back on the number of workers engaged, what will become of employment opportunities as a whole? Is there not an insolvable dilemma between automation and full employment?

The Automation Dilemma: New Products

The superficial answer to this is the simple statement that human wants are unlimited. Stated in this general way (even though we assume it for the moment to be true), it does not quite meet the problem here confronting us. Automation applies mainly, though not quite exclusively, to the production of material goods, and it is the cutback of employment in the area of material goods that I have been talking about. Now can we also say that human wants in the realm of material goods are unlimited? The law of diminishing utility says "no." A degree of satiety is reached sooner or later with respect to every category of material goods. Two chickens in every pot, two cars in every garage—yes, but even so there is a limit. This the neo-classicals did not deny. But the neo-classical answer (apart from the absurdities of Say's law) was that all-round satiety is not reached, because in a progressive society new products are continually being invented, and this staves off the evil day of saturation. Imagine the degree of satiety we should have reached today with respect to durable goods had the automobile not been invented. Invention, new products—this was the neo-classical answer to our conundrum.

Gadgets and Consumer Sovereignty

And to a degree it was a pretty good answer. But it is by now quite evident that it was adequate only up to a point. Once the standard of living has reached the full status of an affluent society—a society in which most people have a radio in every room, TV sets in several rooms, two cars (and often three) in every garage, refrigerators, washing machines, etc., etc., the problem of new products poses a difficulty hitherto unknown. As you go further in the invention of new products, you reach a situation in which more and more the new things contribute little, if at all, to the comforts and conveniences of living. Indeed they may have the opposite effect until a high percentage of income is spent on the repair and maintenance of gadgets. Still gadgets undoubtedly have a certain appeal— adult playthings, so to speak, things that arouse interest and curiosity; and the possession of such gadgets can more or less become an index of social status and prestige. Thus new products, new gadgets, can be pushed far beyond the limits of realism into an area dominated by subtle psychiatric suggestions. The notion must be inculcated into the mind of the buyer that this new plaything is in some sense important. We are here a long, long way from a world of plain living and high thinking. We are in a child's dreamland of playthings and gadgets.

Not long ago one of our leading magazines published a glowing account of "new products." Among other things it presented a photograph of an air-conditioned, glass-encased, motorized lawn mower; there were pocket-size radios, electric door mats, striped tooth paste, an "optichron" flashing the face of a wrist watch on the ceiling, and last, but not least, an underwater walkie-talkie for garrulous skin divers. Yet note the ominous fact that, despite the endless stream of new gadgets, employment in the output of "material things" has reached a ceiling and from here out appears to be on the decline.

These gadgets, these trivialities, are not easily sold. Consumers do not rush out to buy. Witness the currently stepped-up effort on the part of salesmanship to firm up the grip on the consumer's dollar. Advertising outlays in the United States have increased from $1.0 billion in 1921 to $10 billion in 1956 and perhaps $12 billion or more by 1960—a sum roughly equal to two-thirds of the aggregate expenditures on education from kindergarten on through the university.

And this vast effort to hold the line for material goods is taking place just at the time when we so desperately need to use more of our resources for national security and for the accumulated backlog of urgent community needs. A not inconsiderable part of our productive energies is wasted on the business of manufacturing wants, many of which in turn cause diversion of effort away from an optimum allocation of our resources.

Economists used to argue, and some still do, that the consumer in a free price system is entitled to what he wants, foolish though it may be. "Consumer sovereignty" was the phrase.[6] This line of reasoning could indeed claim a good deal of solid validity in the days of free and vigorous competition. In former times price, quality, and durability counted. But it is difficult to see how an economist who has been instructed in

[6] The head of a drug concern, who acknowledged in Senate hearings that his "wonder drug" sold for a price 1,863 per cent higher than the manufacturer's cost, denied that the price was excessive, since it supported medical research to which, he said, the customers must contribute. Consumers are thus subjected to "taxation without representation." See *The New York Times*, December 8, 1959.

the theory of monopolistic competition can still adhere to the consumer-sovereignty dogma. Nowadays consumers no longer act on their own free will. The demand curve is no longer the product of spontaneous wants. It is manufactured. The operating costs of modern corporations relate not merely to the supplying of wants but also to the creation of wants. Social values are created. One comes to feel that mechanical gadgets are more important than schools. Consumer wants are no longer a matter of individual choice. They are mass-produced.

I am continually astonished to hear people talk as though the freedom of our society is somehow infringed upon if educators, writers, or, if you will, "reformers," urge the importance of shifting expenditures toward the public sector. Advertisers may spend billions of dollars in a gigantic effort to direct the flow of expenditures, but a democratic society through a democratically elected government may not do so! Economists who are "crying havoc about too much private expenditures" are playing with fire, says Raymond J. Saulnier, President Eisenhower's chairman of the Council of Economic Advisers, when they propose more and more Federal direction. "Sometimes I get the impression," he said, "that they are talking about a new set of blue laws." [7]

A balanced and highly enlightened view on this matter of consumer sovereignty is expressed in a pamphlet issued by the Committee for Economic Development, "We Can Have Better Schools." We in America, the statement reads, produce "what we as a people say, privately through the market or publicly through government, we want. . . . We have developed a powerful and responsive economy. . . . We also have developed a strong and responsive political system. It produces the government policies that a majority among us wants. These great systems [economic and political] will not, by themselves, create a good society and good lives for most

[7] *The New York Times*, March 21, 1960.

of us. They will produce what is good, desirable and valuable only if we can *decide* what is good, desirable and valuable. . . . A democracy lives or dies by the ability of its people to choose wisely. We need better schools to teach us how to understand the alternatives before us. . . . Schools must help us with the knowledge and the judgment that we need for these great decisions."

Education and leadership—that is the answer. Without these the people perish.

It is a striking fact that the very word "competition" has taken on a new meaning. Competition formerly meant lower prices and better quality. Nowadays it is freely admitted that old-fashioned competition no longer prevails. The concept of competition has changed to that of "rivalry for customers." [8] Competition has become a "titanic struggle to beat each other in the market" by means of intensive and persuasive selling techniques. The competitive struggle runs not in terms of price; it runs in terms of dubious advertising techniques designed to attach customers to a brand name. "Selling" has become a major concern of modern business. "The very fact that, as a whole, the American consuming public has become so rich puts a special burden on the arts of marketing," says Dexter Keezer in his recent book *New Forces in American Business*.[9] No longer is there any compulsion to continue to purchase an expanding volume of material goods.

Consumer "education" operates in two directions, each reinforcing the other. In one direction an immense effort is made to create social values which will build up a demand for gadgets and thus hold the line for the material-goods industries. In another direction an equally strong effort is made to persuade the public that government expenditures should be re-

[8] Dexter M. Keezer, *New Forces in American Business*, McGraw-Hill, 1959, pp. 152–156.
[9] *Ibid.*, p. 241.

duced. We are witnessing, so to speak, a contest between a gadget society and a civilized society.

We have reached a point at which American prosperity (so financial journalists tell us) rests heavily on the continued output of 7 million cars per year. We must keep this treadmill going to employ our labor force—a species of pyramid building. Styling and annual models have paved the way for perpetual prosperity. It is the modern version of the "make-work" philosophy. So we keep adding to our stock of automobiles. Yet we already have enough cars to take the entire population of the United States, Great Britain, and Germany out for a "Sunday buggy ride," if you please, with only five persons (babies included) in each car. No shortage of supply here!

Poverty and Unsatisfied Wants

To a degree governmental policy itself can justifiably enlarge the scope of the material-goods sector. Even in our opulent society there is still a considerable section of our population (possibly 20 per cent) which is too poor to provide itself with the material goods it needs. Mere aggregate growth in the economy as a whole or mere increases in the average real income of Americans generally will not cure this situation. A rich country like the United States should once and for all wipe out poverty. To do so would cost us relatively little. It means more education for the submerged fifth, better housing, better medical care, a higher minimum wage, more adequate unemployment and old-age insurance, aid to distressed areas, rehabilitation, and retraining. An adequate program would open up a considerable new market for material goods and thereby soften the relative decline of this sphere of activity.

Services

Still we have not exhausted the neo-classical answer to the conundrum of automation and declining employment in the material-goods sector. The first answer, as we have seen, is new products—products that really raise the standard of living. The second answer is gadgets and the creation of social values that make these gadgets seem important. The third is an investment in the education and health of the lowest quintile of our population and a more equitable distribution of income. The increased buying power of this poorest sector could enlarge somewhat the market for material goods. But if all these will not suffice, as appears currently to be the case, then the answer is services. In fact this has been the answer during the last decade. Employment in the area of material goods has reached a plateau and perhaps started on a decline, but employment has rapidly expanded in the service fields. Indeed in the ten years from 1947 to 1957 employment in trade increased 23 per cent, finance 40 per cent, service 32 per cent, and public service 39 per cent. And so, despite the decline in employment in the production of material goods, we have enjoyed a sufficient increase in the service field, public and private, to provide substantially full employment.

The shift, relatively speaking, from material goods to services, public and private, has important implications for the business community. Private enterprise is amazingly efficient in the production of material goods and in the proliferation of new products. As living standards rise, however, physical wants become more and more satiated, though this process is slowed down a good deal by the introduction of new products and new gadgets. The affluent society becomes, as far as physical goods are concerned, a gadget society in which the necessities of life and the really useful things are taken for granted. At this stage there is at least the possibility that human wants will turn increasingly to cultural, intellectual, recreational, and community activities. Many important service industries can adequately and satisfactorily be carried on by private enterprise. And to a considerable extent private enterprise can and does contribute to the recreational, educational, health, and cultural needs of a highly advanced society. But it is quite evident that, despite opposition, the handwriting on the wall points out a rapidly growing role of government in all these areas. Many people still attempt, but I am sure with little success, to close their eyes to this inexorable fact. The progress we shall make toward a truly higher standard of living in the next few decades will depend above all upon the degree to which we choose to use the vast powers of a democratic government to build a really civilized community.

Our Accumulating Public Needs

We have allowed our social plant to run down. I am not speaking here of new programs, however much needed they may be. I am referring to conventional and long-established community services. Even here we have not been holding our own.

The *New York Times*, referring to the problems that are overwhelming all our great metropolitan centers, quoted the familiar phrase from *Through the Looking-Glass*: "Now, *here*, you see," said the Queen to Alice, "it takes all the running you can do, to keep in the same place. If you want to get somewhere else, you must run at least twice as fast as that." Urban needs pile up—slum clearance, hospitals, libraries, recreational facilities, renovations, and new construction. The city's apparatus grows obsolescent overnight. "There is no end in sight," says the *Times*, "for New York or any other city." Large-scale transit improvements; new schools to replace those that are quite obsolete or seriously inadequate and high schools for neighborhoods that have no high schools at all; new hospitals; a construction program for sewage-treatment plants adequate to protect the bathing beaches from contamination are needed. The backlog dating first from the Great Depression and then from the Second World War has resulted in serious obsolescence and deterioration in the physical plant of urban communities. Deficiencies are piling up. To delay action now will only aggravate the problem and increase the ultimate costs.

The great Metropolitan Museum of Art, which had maintained the proud tradition of being open to the public every day of the week for nearly seventy years, was forced in the summer of 1959 to close every Monday—and this at a time when the population of the city of New York was never more prosperous. The attendance of visitors has greatly increased. There is no lack of interest, and yet the funds have not been made available to do for the public what had been done for seventy years. Public-library branches have reduced their open hours. Formerly all the city's libraries were open from 9 A.M. to 9 P.M., but now the hours have been sharply reduced. Adult-education sessions have been reduced. The custodial and teaching staff of the Museum of Natural History has been sharply reduced. With 5,000 requests for guided tours for school children, only 1,300 could be accommodated.

The New York Commissioner of Hospitals painted a grim picture of shortages of nurses in municipal hospitals and health work, due to inadequate pay scales. The Department of Health, the Deputy Commissioner has stated, has only two-thirds as many nurses now as a decade ago, despite the need for an expanded program. Crime and violence have made whole areas unsafe. It was reported in the *New York Times* that from January to October, 1959, more than 470 taxi drivers had been assaulted or robbed or both. Many taxi drivers refuse to take fares into "problem neighborhoods." It is generally said that one cannot safely enter Central Park after dark. All this in the richest urban community in the world, and the record in other large metropolitan centers is by and large no better, and often even worse.

The number of juvenile-delinquency cases handled by the courts has increased since 1940 in the country as a whole 2.7-fold per capita for children ten to seventeen years old. Inadequate schooling, inadequate housing, inadequate recreational facilities, social tensions, the increasing strains of congested urban living, and many other subtle and little-understood factors all play a role. Using the term in its broadest sense, what is needed most of all to lift our society out of this morass is education. One cannot fail to ask, says Dr. James R. Kilian, Jr., "whether we Americans, in our drive to make and acquire things, have not given too little attention to developing men and ideas."

If we were a poor country, that would be one thing. But here we are, the richest country in the world, with the highest real income per capita in our entire history and in the history of the human race. We have got ourselves into a frame of mind which permits this "affluence in private goods" and at the same time this "poverty which afflicts us in public services." [10] This frame of mind has not just happened. It has been assiduously cultivated. Yet its roots lie deep. We are living in a tumultuous age—an age of disillusionment. The World War, the Korean conflict, the cold war. We are trying to escape from reality. We do not like to face the cold facts of the world we live in. We are caught up in a wave of escapism and comfortable complacency.

Whatever the web of causal factors, the plain fact is that private wealth has increased while public services have failed

[10] J. K. Galbraith, *The Affluent Society*, Houghton Mifflin, 1958, p. 240.

to keep pace with our accumulations of material things. We have been building pyramids on a gigantic scale. In the midst of a great world crisis we profess to believe that our way of life, our freedoms, our institutions will be destroyed unless we pursue business-as-usual policies. We devise more and more gadgets to keep our treadmill actively going.

Growth for What?

We have had much public discussion, in recent years, about the possibility of accelerating our rate of growth from the historical 3 per cent to perhaps 4½ or 5 per cent. It is evident that this rate cannot easily be achieved. It will require a determined effort to strengthen our educational system, to train and retrain our several million unemployed, the vast majority of whom are unskilled and therefore unfit for modern industry. It will require a substantial increase in our annual crop of first-class scientists. It will require an expanded program of basic research. It will require a large public investment in both our human and natural resources.

And once the enlarged capacity to produce goods and services begins to bear fruit, what shall it be used for?

Disarmament and Released Resources

Consider another possibility. Let us suppose that productive resources might within the next decade be set free through universal and total disarmament. What should we use this released productive capacity for?

I do not here raise the often-debated question: Would total disarmament mean vast unemployment? About this there is by now no serious disagreement, at least among professional economists. Adequate aggregate demand sufficient to provide full employment is fairly easily within our reach. We are pretty firmly confident that we know what to do. The really difficult problem is not how to achieve and maintain full employment. The problem about which there is likely to be the greatest disagreement is rather the use to which our newly released productive resources shall be put.

Growth of Public Budgets

The expansion of public services will mean a growth in public budgets in relation to the Gross National Product. This has been going on for a long time and it will continue. Federal expenditures (defense expenditures excluded) increased 2.5 times as fast as the GNP in the United States from 1929 to 1959. In the United Kingdom governmental expenditures (after deducting defense and war-related expenditures) increased 3.5 times faster than the GNP from 1900 to 1955. All over the free world this tendency is evident.[11]

The Role of Private Enterprise

We are developing more and more a dual society—a joint partnership of private enterprise and government. In this joint partnership private enterprise produces virtually all the ma-

[11] It is an error to assume that mere growth in the GNP will automatically provide additional sources of funds for an expansion of public services. In so far as the increase in GNP is due to population growth, such increase can only *maintain* per capita income. And if the increase in GNP does represent an increase in *per capita* real income, such gains may well be restricted wholly or mainly to the private sector, since productivity advances are difficult to achieve in the service area. If money wages rise as fast as productivity, costs in the public sector for the *same* amount of services will rise. And so the same *percentage* of the larger GNP will have to be tapped in order to provide the same amount of public services. To achieve an increase in public services would call for an *increased* percentage allocation of GNP to public uses.

terial goods. Even in the socialist countries of Western Europe, notably the Scandinavian countries, the old Marxian dogma of government ownership of the means of production has been discarded. Social democratic parties have dominated the governments of Sweden, Denmark, and Norway for well-nigh a whole generation. These socialist governments have not undertaken any extensive nationalization of any industry. True, railroads and public utilities and public power projects are government-owned and government-operated, but all that was introduced by conservative governments long before the socialists came into power. The Scandinavian countries do not want any extension of government ownership. Instead they want the welfare state. Private enterprise produces the goods. But it is the function of the government to provide a growing part of the community services and facilities that are essential for a high standard of civilization and culture. This is the meaning of the welfare state.

The British Labor party is gradually learning, though it has been rather slow to learn, the lesson which the Scandinavian countries learned long ago—namely, that private enterprise can do a better job in the operation of industry than can the government. The British Labor party has been slow in getting rid of obsolete Marxian dogmas. But it is coming on. In the last election it soft-pedaled the issue of nationalization. And its defeat at the polls indicates that this issue from here out cannot again be revived. On the other hand, the Conservative party has boldly supported the program of the welfare state. The class war, said Macmillan after the election, is no longer an issue in Great Britain. The Labor party is indeed more aggressive, but both parties are committed to the welfare state, and private enterprise need no longer fear any serious attack on its hold on the means of production. In West Germany the Social Democratic party met on November 13, 1959, to bury its agelong program of nationalization of industry. It adopted a new manifesto which declared that the private ownership of the means of production may justly claim the protection of society.

The Role of Education

For a long time to come our community needs will be so imperative, for the accumulated backlog is so great, that there need be no fear that we cannot usefully employ our labor force. But in order to serve the needs of the highly civilized welfare state, the labor force will need to be an educated labor force. Even in the material-goods sector, the trained technicians are wanted in increasing numbers, while operatives are on the decline. From 1947 to 1957 the number of professional and technical personnel increased 75 per cent, other white-collar groups increased 30 per cent, while aggregate employment, including the rapidly growing groups already mentioned, increased only 11 per cent. To train the labor force for the advanced society that modern technology has made possible will obviously require a gigantic educational operation. This alone will demand an increased role of government. Mass education in a really meaningful sense—not the mere ability to write a slovenly letter or read the sports section of the newspaper—is a long way off, and I have no doubt that many people, perhaps most, think that it can't be achieved. Yet there is an enormous untapped demand in this country for adult education—for classes in literature, history, science, art, languages, economics, philosophy, comparative government. Centers of adult education are provided with incredibly meager facilities—congested and obsolete buildings, inadequate teaching staff. The salary scales are unbelievably low. I happen to know, because I have served for some years on the board of an adult-education center.

The masses *can* be culturally educated. The typical Italian worker can sing large sections of almost all the great Italian operas. Even relatively small towns in Denmark have art museums. School symphonies and dramatic performances, when cultivated, can flourish on an incredibly wide scale from junior high school up. We have already demonstrated this in our own country. The adult-education centers disclose a widespread demand for liberal arts courses. The notion that the population generally is incapable of cultural interests and cultural activities is belied by the almost universal spread of craftsmanship throughout the Middle Ages and in the early modern period. Is it not strange that it is peculiarly in our modern democracies, with their universal suffrage, that we have no real faith in mass education? A gigantic educational reawakening, scientific and cultural, is the first order of the day. Says Vice Admiral Rickover: "Our really great race with the Soviet Union is in education. Unless we in the United States can solve our educational problems, we will have difficulty in solving other problems."

President Eisenhower's Science Advisory Committee, which made its report to the President in May, 1959, stated that we are now spending in the aggregate almost $18 billion per year, all the way from kindergarten on up through college and university. This amounts to a little less than 4 per cent of our Gross National Product. The Committee's recommendation called for a doubling of this amount, or an increase of $18 billion, raising the total to $36 billion per year. This amount, the Committee stated, was needed even on the minimum basis of national security, to say nothing about meeting the cultural needs of a great society. Upon making the report public, the President offered no suggestion as to how it might be implemented. He said it was a good report and he hoped many people would read it!

The great job of education lies before us. We have allowed the greatest potential educational media of all times—the TV and the radio—to slip out of our grasp. Some 42 million homes are tuned in to TV on an average night, and the average TV set is in use 5.2 hours per day. It is no exaggeration to say that the television, the radio, and the movie have become so influential as educational media that they rival the influence of the public school system itself. And the programs are controlled not by educators but by salesmen. We have allowed the TV to seek the lowest denominator. The net effect is to pull down even the upper strata until a cumulative downward movement depresses the general cultural, moral, and social values of the whole society. There is a law of social values, not unlike Gresham's law in economics, about bad money driving out good money.

The editor of *Harper's Magazine* has suggested that a central authority should be set up to produce public-service programs on TV. This appeared shocking to the president of the Columbia Broadcasting System. He professes to believe that television must reflect the current values of the society it serves. It cannot, he says, create these values. For him the all-important question is how much light diversion 50 million people want in their leisure hours.

In the language of the TV sponsors themselves, it is the crime and violence shows and the westerns that "give you the most for your money."

Says Telford Taylor, formerly general counsel to the FCC and more recently with the Joint Council on Education and Television: "It is advertising's monopoly of financial support of television that makes television programs what they are today. He who pays the piper calls the tune, even when he pays with other people's money. That is why . . . television will remain at or about its present level of quality as long as it is financially based exclusively on advertising." [12]

[12] *The New York Times,* December 4, 1959.

What kind of people we are and what kind of society we will build depend in no small measure upon the things that are pressed in on our minds day by day over the radio and television. This is especially true because the radio and the television, unlike all other means of communication and entertainment, invade the privacy of the home.

Perhaps the answer is pay TV. Perhaps the answer is federally subsidized programs controlled by an Educational and Cultural Authority. Perhaps the answer is the complete incorporation of the whole TV system into a Federal Department of Public Education. This in effect is what we have in some European countries and to a degree in Canada. I repeat once again, if the service area is to be expanded as fast as automation proves able to release manpower from the production of material goods, the first all-important job is a vast expansion of public education, including adult education. This is basic to everything else—recreation, use of leisure time, and the problems related to our ever-growing aged population. Leisure without education can be a curse.

One Hundred Honors High Schools

Most people agree that the standard of instruction in our high schools is far below what it might be. I suggest that one way to buoy up our secondary education would be to establish a hundred federally financed pilot high schools scattered throughout the country. To ensure that each geographical section was fairly served, we might place eight in each Federal Reserve District. Federally financed competitive scholarships, adequate to cover all expenses, should be awarded to the ablest students in each district. Such a program would serve to tap brains that now are allowed to run waste. It would swell the number of gifted students entering our universities. And these "honor high schools" would become models for all the rest, thereby raising the standard of high school instruction throughout the country.

Federally Financed College and University Scholarships

Tuitions, especially in private colleges and universities, have already reached a point at which higher education is scarcely within the reach of even middle-class incomes. This situation is, to be sure, softened somewhat by college and university scholarship grants based on need. Nevertheless our best private colleges and universities are fast becoming—indeed already are —high-income, upper-class institutions. Without a broadly based system of federally financed scholarships the future of our great private educational institutions is not bright.

We are here confronted with a real danger to our democratic society, based as it is on the principle of equality of opportunity. We are not drawing into our great universities, public or private, the most gifted youth throughout the length and breadth of the land and from all income classes.

Sometimes it is said that greater expenditures on education— higher teachers' salaries, more buildings—will not of themselves ensure real educational progress. Higher salaries and more schools we must have. But we must also strike out on new lines. And how could we spend money more wisely than to build and operate a hundred honors high schools and provide a program of federally financed scholarships for gifted students?

The American ideal is based on public schools. Especially in the east, the public school is generally inferior to the better private schools. This is not a healthy situation for a democratic society. Equality of opportunity demands that this double standard be eliminated.

A Council of Social Values

I have one more concrete suggestion to make.[18] We have our Employment Act of 1946, which gave us a Council of Economic Advisers, the annual *Economic Report of the President*, and the annual *Report of the Joint Economic Committee of the Congress*. This bit of social machinery, social engineering, is of the greatest importance. I propose that we now set up, by act of Congress, a Council of Social Values. This act should require the President each year, aided by this council, to report to the Congress and to the people on our cultural gains and losses. The President should be required to point out how far we have fallen short, during the past year, of the goals previously proclaimed. He should be required to set forth goals for the coming year and to indicate the programs and policies necessary to achieve these goals. Is it not remarkable that, having reached our currently high standard of abundance with respect to material goods, we still talk and act very much as though these were our only concern? Is it not high time that we begin to devote in our State of the Union message some attention to the cultural needs of an advanced society? A Council of Social Values could help at least in some measure to redress the present unequal emphasis on material things. It would help to solve the dilemma of automation and pyramid building.

John D. Rockefeller III, in a recent speech on "Support of Arts as a Public Duty," said: "The box office alone can never

[18] After writing this, I read in the *New York Times* a letter from former Senator William Benton in which he referred to a proposal made by him while he was a member of Congress, calling for a permanent commission provided with a budget and a staff to launch studies and issue a report on radio and TV each year.

See also in this connection my "Standards and Values in a Rich Society," in *The American Economy*, McGraw-Hill, 1957, chap. 8.

support the arts any more than hospital bills can cover all hospital costs or tuition fees the full cost of education." Creative fulfillment, he said, is as important today to man's well-being and happiness as his need for better physical health was fifty years ago. The arts have become, he said, an important means for Americans to gain fulfillment in their new leisure time. "It is a responsibility of the whole community, business, foundations, individual citizens, and government." [14]

[14] *The New York Times*, October 7, 1959.

CHAPTER 8

FINANCING THE DUAL ECONOMY

In the last chapter I discussed at some length the partnership which I believe to be increasingly necessary between private enterprise and government. The role of private enterprise is now, and will continue to be, primarily that of producing a rich and varied supply of material goods. Owing to automation, however, employment in the material-goods sector is declining. Employment in the service area is rising. And just as private enterprise serves best in the material-goods sector, so government serves best to satisfy our cultural needs. The role of government will increasingly be that of providing a wide range of services—those services which we have come to associate with the welfare state—social security, health, housing, education, recreation and cultural programs, and community projects.

The further we move into the Dual Economy, the more we shall encounter two problems: (1) the availability of funds for private capital formation and for industrial research and (2) the "shrinking tax base" as the government sector grows larger and larger relative to the private sector. Where is the money coming from to keep the Dual Economy going?

Financing Private Investment in the Dual Economy

Consider first the sources of private investment funds. During the last few decades, and with accelerated speed since the Second World War, we have been moving farther and farther into new territory as far as the sources of investment funds are concerned.

Formerly such funds came primarily from stock subscriptions, bond issues, and bank loans. More recently investment funds have come primarily from internal sources, namely, retained profits, depletion allowances, depreciation, and amortization charges. From 1955 to 1959 inclusive $138.2 billion came from internal sources while only $58.2 billion came from bank loans, mortgage loans, and new issues of securities.

In the earlier stages of development profits were necessarily rather meager, and so relatively little reliance could be placed on retained earnings as a source of funds. One had to look outside of the enterprise itself for investment funds. Capitalists and banks had to be found that were willing to assume risks and advance the funds necessary to start new enterprises. In the earlier stages of our history as an industrial nation, depreciation allowances played only a small role in new capital financing. The aggregate accumulated stock of plant and equipment subject to depreciation was small. Moreover depreciation accounting had not developed to any high degree of expertness.

Equally important is the fact that, in the days when numerous producing units occupied each industrial field, prices and profits were controlled by competition. Retained earnings could not be "planned" to the degree that is possible under oligopolistic and quasi-monopolistic conditions. In the recent drug hearings in Washington corporation heads testified that fantastically high markups were deliberately made in order to provide ample money for research.

Prior to the advent of "administered" prices, funds for research or for investment in plant and equipment were more dependent upon the capital markets and on borrowings from banks. Savings and bank credit were the primary sources of investment funds. But now funds for investment may be tapped from consumers via high administered prices bolstered by high-pressure advertising. As far as outlays on research are concerned, this is all the more true since the tax reforms of 1954 permit research outlays to be deductible as current expense.[1] Under this procedure research outlays are made a part of cost to be covered by an adequate price. Prior to 1954 such outlays were regarded as a long-term investment, deductible over a period of years.

When investment funds are obtained from the capital market, those who supply the funds have a voice in the business. In the final analysis stockholders control, and banks and bondholders have at least a contingent voice. In any event they are paid dividends and interest for their participation. But nowadays the consumer, via the administered pricing system, pays a price sufficiently high to cover current research outlays and depreciation allowances, and in addition sufficiently high prices to provide profits not only for dividend payments but also for adequate retained earnings. This is taxation without representation.

It is said that about one-half of total medical research in the United States is paid by the Federal government, one-fourth by universities, and one-fourth by drug manufacturers. Government research is paid by taxes imposed by an elected Congress. The taxpayers elect the legislators who vote the appropriations. But the consumer who pays prices which are

[1] It is not impossible that the system of accelerated depreciation may tend to cause higher administered prices, since there is a tendency to fix prices at some markup percentage above costs. Accelerated depreciation raises the costs in the earlier stages of the life of fixed capital assets.

higher than necessary to cover costs (including normal or "competitive" profits) is in the final analysis the one who supplies the funds which are plowed back into businesses operating under the system of administered prices.

The average annual investment made by *corporations* in plant, equipment, and inventories in the period 1955 to 1959 inclusive was $31.0 billion. Internal sources (retained earnings, depreciation, amortization, and depletion allowances) averaged in this period $27.6 billion. Internal sources were therefore sufficient to finance exactly 90 per cent of the aggregate investment in *fixed capital and inventories combined.* Outside sources of funds (bank loans, mortgage loans, and new issues) were tapped to cover the remaining 10 per cent and to finance net accumulations of cash, securities, and net receivables.

Depreciation and amortization allowances now supply two-thirds of the funds spent by corporations on plant and equipment. Depreciation allowances have been increased not only by more generous tax treatment, but also by the fact that an enormous amount of new corporate plants and producers' equipment have been built in recent years (postwar backlog and new techniques). This vast accumulation of new productive facilities is generating a huge volume of depreciation allowances. And the fact that so much of the plant and equipment is new means that replacement is a long way off. Accordingly the depreciation funds can immediately be used, not for replacement, but for net additions to the stock of fixed capital. And those new capital assets, in turn, are again subject to depreciation. In a growing society you are always ahead of the game. Depreciation allowances tend to exceed replacement expenditures.[2] In 1955–1959 an annual volume of nearly $19 billion of corporate depreciation funds was available for investment, and currently it amounts to nearly $23 billion. In

[2] However, in a rising-price period there is likely to be a lag in the adjustment of depreciation charges to the cost of replacement.

addition there are the retained corporate earnings, amounting in 1955–1959 to $9 billion per year.

We have thus reached a new, and perhaps necessary, stage in financing private investment. Without this development it is doubtful if we could have obtained the investment funds needed for growth and expansion. Clearly, however, this development raises questions with respect to governmental supervision or control.

Financing the Government in the Dual Economy

And now the question: Where is the tax money coming from if the private-enterprise base, though growing absolutely, is undergoing a relative decline?

Unless one has given considerable thought to this question, the instinctive answer is that private enterprise is the only true source of income. All incomes, so it is argued, are derived directly or indirectly from private enterprise. Governments obtain their income, it is said, from private enterprise. This works all right as long as the government sector is relatively small. But what will happen, it is asked, should the government sector grow and grow in relation to the private sector? Will not the true source of funds, under these circumstances, eventually dry up?

Frequently one hears the comment that the payrolls of private industry are the source of the whole national income, that government is supported by business, that private enterprise alone is productive.[3]

Here we can learn from the early classical economists. Adam Smith introduced a novel idea into economics—a new concept of productivity. The physiocrats had held the view that agriculture alone was productive. Agriculture supplied the neces-

[3] Cf. Alvin H. Hansen, *Fiscal Policy and Business Cycles*, Norton, 1941, pp. 146–152.

sities of life for the agricultural population, and if there was a surplus left over, it was possible out of this "net product" to support the "unproductive" town population.

It is not difficult to see how the physiocratic concept of productivity was born out of the conditions emerging from the Middle Ages. Towns originally were simply the winter residences of great feudal lords. The town population grew up around the court. It performed personal services, prepared food, made rich clothing and ornaments, jewels, laces, velvets, tapestries, clocks, and furniture. All this activity was supported and sustained from the surplus which the lord was able to draw from his agricultural domain. Without this surplus, life in the town would quickly ebb away. The town had no independent source of subsistence. It drew its sustenance from the country.

Town life was a luxury which could only be supported out of a richly productive countryside. Town life could develop only so far as an agricultural surplus could be produced and, through feudal rights and privileges, drawn off from the land to enrich the town life of the landed aristocracy. If king and country were to become rich and powerful, it was necessary to encourage agriculture. Agriculture alone was really productive. All other pursuits were sterile and unproductive. This was the doctrine of the physiocrats.

The thesis that agriculture was the fountainhead of all wealth, that agricultural pursuits alone were productive, was once and for all disposed of in Adam Smith's great book *The Wealth of Nations*. The view he challenged had seemed so self-evident and plausible that none had seriously questioned it, precisely as is the case today with respect to the role of government. Yet increasingly, as manufacture and trade developed, it was inevitable that sooner or later it would become apparent to an original mind that the old thesis simply did not fit the facts of a more highly developed society.

The opening paragraph in *The Wealth of Nations* strikes directly at the fallacy of the *produit net* philosophy. Smith regarded labor, not agriculture, as the basic source of wealth. Through division of labor and exchange, productivity is increased. If one exchanges one's agricultural surplus against the products of specialized and efficient town craftsmen, one increases one's own product. Exchange with the town enriches the country.

Now, in point of fact, this analysis did not represent merely a new interpretation of the same facts. To some extent the facts themselves had changed. At the earliest emergence of town life, the town, as we have noted, was simply a collection of families catering to the wants of the lord and his court. It had no independent existence. The activities of the town represented the lord's method of consuming his agricultural surplus.

But gradually some of the mechanics of the town acquired an independent status of their own. They offered their own wares in exchange. Country barons and squires exchanged their agricultural surpluses for the products of the town's craftsmen. Thus a real exchange developed between country and town.

The breakdown of feudal privileges in the French Revolution developed and expanded this exchange process. The peasant, having acquired a new status, was in a stronger position to retain control over his surplus product. By the time the development of social institutions had reached this point, it was possible to recognize that the country no longer supported the town any more than the town supported the country. It was no longer meaningful to say that agriculture was productive while manufacture was not, or even that agriculture was more productive than manufacture. Both activities satisfied human wants.

But while Adam Smith freed the thinking of his time from

the physiocrats' narrow concept of productivity, he failed to liberate himself and his generation wholly from the basic physiocratic error. While urging that manufacturing was equally as productive as agriculture, he nevertheless held that only those workers engaged in making material goods were really productive. Thus, he argued that not only menial servants, but also churchmen, lawyers, physicians, men of letters of all kinds, players, musicians, opera singers, etc., were unproductive laborers. It is remarkable that, once he had taken the first step in the right direction, he should have made this error. If manufacture is productive, since it no less than agriculture satisfies human wants, surely the opera singer, the physician, the teacher are equally productive. At a later stage in economic thinking the logic of Adam Smith's own position, which he imperfectly applied, was pointed out and universally accepted by all economists.

But the logic of this thesis is frequently challenged with respect to governmental expenditures. Public investments (parks, roads, playgrounds, hospitals), it is often asserted, are in some sense unproductive; only private capital expenditures are regarded as productive.

In discussing the productiveness of private business expenditures, it is important to make a sharp distinction between (1) the creation of a flow of real income of goods or services and (2) the creation of new instruments of production which increase the efficiency of labor and result in a larger flow of real income than might otherwise be possible. The former is a utility-creating expenditure; the latter is an efficiency-creating expenditure. Investment which duplicates existing plants in accordance with the requirements of growth (as, for example, the erection of another shoe factory) is of the former type. Investment in improved machinery is of the latter type.

The view that public investment is unproductive, while private investment is productive, will not withstand careful analysis. Public investment, like private investment, may be simply utility-creating or it may be also efficiency-creating. The development of a public park, swimming pool, playground, or concert hall makes possible a flow of real income no less than the erection of a shoe factory. Public investment in natural resources or in the construction of school buildings may contribute to raise the efficiency of labor no less than private investment in improved machinery. Public investment, like private investment, if wisely made, may be utility-creating or both utility-creating and efficiency-creating. And in addition to being (1) utility-creating and (2) efficiency-creating, public expenditures no less than private expenditures are also (3) income-creating in the sense that they tend to expand aggregate income and employment.

It is sometimes said that there is an important difference between business expenditures and governmental expenditures, in that the former are self-sustaining while the latter are not. But this will not withstand careful scrutiny. No private business can sustain its sales volume unless the outlays of other businesses or the government continue to feed the income stream. The sales receipts of private business, no less than the tax receipts of government, depend upon the maintenance of a high national income. And the outlays of government can and do contribute to a sustained national income, no less than the outlays of private business. Indeed, when private business outlays decline, the government may be the only agency that is in a position to go forward and sustain the national income through increased expenditures.

When it is said that public expenditures are "sustained out of" private income, it will be disclosed, on careful analysis, that the reasoning is precisely similar to that of the physiocrats. Manufactures were sustained, it was said, out of the surplus product of agriculture. The true fact, however, was that the real income of the community was raised enormously by diverting a part of the productive resources to manufactures. In like manner, under modern conditions, many wants can be satisfied only by governmental action, and in other cases more effectively by governmental action. Roads, streets, sewage disposal, reforestation, flood control, parks, schools, public health, hospitals, low-cost housing, social insurance, public playgrounds, and other recreational and cultural facilities—all these represent ways of enlarging our real income far beyond what it could be if these things were not undertaken by government. These activities are utility-creating and in part efficiency-creating, no less than the activities of private enterprise. The governmental expenditures are not supported out of private enterprise any more than manufacture is supported out of the agricultural surplus. Just as the manufacturing population buys the surplus of agriculture in exchange for its products, so also the services of government enter into the exchange process and enrich the income stream. It is true that part of the exchange payment is in the form of taxes, but this fact in no way alters the fundamental fact of exchange. In this process of exchange it is not true that any one segment of the exchange economy supports any other segment. Manufacturing is not maintained out of the surplus of agriculture, and government is not maintained out of the surplus of private enterprise. Each segment contributes to the total flow of real income, and each takes its share out of the income stream either by charging a price or by collecting a tax. Outlays create incomes and incomes cover costs.

In the sense that the most essential necessity of life—food—is produced by agriculture, it may be said that agriculture is basic to all other economic activity. This seems to give it a sort of priority. But this priority has a meaning only in primitive societies where it is necessary to devote all, or nearly all, of productive resources to the procurement of food. As a society becomes more productive, agriculture loses its right of priority.

The very superabundance of agricultural products implies that more emphasis must be placed upon other economic pursuits. Manufacture, indeed, may now become the really important branch in that its products are relatively scarce in relation to the products of agriculture. In an agricultural-surplus society manufactures may assert a certain claim to priority.

The same analysis applies to governmental activities: Once society becomes surfeited with material goods, public needs demand prior consideration.

I have discussed the problem of income creation, and I have tried to show that the employment of productive resources, whether by government or by private enterprise, involves the payment of money incomes to the employed factors of production. And the income thus paid out is sufficient to buy back all the goods and services produced. Whether this "purchase" comes about via the price-tag mechanism or via taxes is from this standpoint quite immaterial. The costs of production are in fact the income receipts of the factors of production. Incomes spring from costs, and expenditures (whether via the price tag or via taxes) spring from income. Costs, income, expenditures—the circle is complete. It is Schumpeter's circular-flow economy.

The publicly provided goods and services are either produced directly under government management or else they are purchased by the government from private producers. Government management could mean either a department like the Post Office Department or a government corporation like the TVA or the Export-Import Bank or the Commodity Credit Corporation. Government purchase of goods and services from private business is illustrated by contract construction work or by the vast governmental purchases of military equipment from private corporations. But whether the government itself produces the goods and services or buys them under contract from private parties, the net effect, as far as income creation is concerned, is the same. Money is paid out which goes into the pockets of individuals, whether wage or salaried workers, or stockholders of the private corporations that do contract work for the government. The entire cost[4] of production is paid out in this manner. The government in its turn recovers the costs thus incurred either by selling the goods and services to the public at a price or else by collecting the cost of their services from the public by means of taxation.

Income Taxes versus Sales Taxes

Omitting the distressing variety of nuisance taxes, special forms of business taxes and excises, custom duties, and the like, there are three main forms of taxes: (1) taxes on property or wealth, (2) taxes on personal and corporate incomes, and (3) taxes on expenditures, whether a general expenditure tax or a specific expenditure tax applied to the purchase of specific goods. Formerly taxes on property dominated. Later the income tax acquired the leading role, and more recently we appear to be moving into sales taxes. At all levels of government income taxes (excluding social security) currently yield revenues amounting to $65 billion; sales taxes of all kinds, $25 billion; and property taxes, $15 billion.

Taxes, however, are not merely ways of raising revenue. Income taxes constitute an important method of redistributing income, and sales taxes alter the market-determined relative-price ratios. Purchase taxes, as the British call them, or sales taxes, as we call them, are unique in that they ride on the coattails, so to speak, of the price tags that are already set in the market place. If they are attached to a price tag, you pay or not, according to your own volition, precisely as in the case

[4] "Cost" here includes the share received by stockholders in the form of profits, whether retained earnings or distributed as dividends. Stockholders no less than salaried officials and workers are included in the concept "factors of production."

of the price tag itself. Now the further we move into the welfare state, the more significant I believe will this particular device for covering government outlays become.

Experience shows that the income tax can be carried to very high percentage figures without seriously interfering with incentives. It is agreed by almost all economists, however, that the present high marginal rates are either ineffective or discriminating and ought to be cut. There are limits, not always easily discernible, to everything. There can be no doubt that the income tax could be pushed up to levels at which incentives would be seriously weakened. Thus far at any rate, there appears to be no evidence that the income taxes in the United States have reached that point. As far as workers are concerned, voluntary refusal to work is nowhere in evidence. By and large a man either has a job or he hasn't. Here it is not a question of withholding marginal increments of effort or labor. If he has a job, the pace is set by the factory production system. The employment figures do not indicate that the tax system prevents people from taking and holding jobs, and the productivity figures do not indicate any slackening of work effort. With respect to extra jobs over and above the regular job, high tax rates, instead of restricting effort, may in fact induce more effort, as in the case of a colleague who announced that the income tax had made such inroads on his disposable income that he was compelled to accept a summer teaching post. In the United States, in high employment periods, hundreds of thousands hold down two jobs to a degree quite unprecedented in our history. Moreover high income taxes, as far as we can see, have not had any unfavorable effect on private investment. For the twelve-year period 1948 to 1959 inclusive, the average ratio of private investment to Gross National Product was equal to that of any previous boom year in our history.

No doubt one can find cases in which work assignments and extra work opportunities are refused on the ground that, after deducting the higher marginal tax rate, the net reward is not deemed worth the extra effort. How far a broadly based income tax can be carried I do not profess to know. We have, however, no doubt reached a point at which we must be mindful of the incentive effect.

Purely for purposes of analysis, in order to see more clearly the limitations involved, let us imagine a situation in which all goods and services are provided by government. Mind you, this need not mean that the government produces most of the goods and services itself. As in the case of military equipment for defense, the government might purchase from private enterprise many of the goods and services which it makes available to the public. Even in the case of the social security transfer payments the recipients use the money so received to buy goods produced by private enterprise. In the situation I am here imagining, private enterprise might conceivably be producing a major part of all the goods and services. But the government, we assume, purchases all the goods and services and makes them available to the public either at a price or as free goods.

Money income, we assume, is paid out either indirectly through private enterprise or directly by the government to the productive factors employed—wages, salaries, dividends. Assume that the government takes back the whole of this income in income taxes. Obviously the thing has become an absurdity. It has become purely a ritual. The income payments made by private enterprise and the government to the employed factors, the taxing of this income by the government, and finally the payment of the tax receipts by the government back to private enterprise and to its own employees has become mere hocus-pocus. Monetary reward for work done will have lost all incentive effect if one can buy nothing. Monetary income means nothing unless there is a price system.

If, in our abstract illustration, the government (instead of making the goods and services freely available to everybody) had placed a price tag upon them, the whole picture would be changed. The price tag restores incentives and makes unequal monetary rewards again meaningful. (We exclude from consideration here the system of distributing goods and services directly without the intermediary of money payments.) Money payments can have no meaning unless the price tag applies to a large part of the available goods and services. The price system is a *sine qua non*. Without it monetary compensation can provide no incentive for efficiency.

Price Tags versus Taxes

Now this purely abstract analysis obviously has a bearing upon two highly important matters. First, there is the problem of the relative merits of government employing the price-tag method to finance its costs as opposed to the tax method. The more the government applies the price-tag method, the more is the price mechanism made available for the maintenance of incentives. Secondly, in the event that the tax method is employed, there remains the problem of which tax to apply: (1) the sales tax or (2) the income tax. The sales tax is attached to market price tags and so preserves the price mechanism. The sales tax is a kind of hybrid between a price system and a tax system. The income tax finances freely available, publicly provided goods and services. Once voted by the Congress, it is compulsory and leaves no choice to the consumer.

Suppose the services offered by government constitute a large proportion of the aggregate goods and services, say 40 or even 50 per cent. We have already gone sufficiently far along the road toward a really opulent society so that percentages of this sort no longer seem ridiculous even though they lie considerably beyond the figure already reached—around 25 per cent. We have gone far enough to know that automation can carry the production of material goods to a point at which the bulk of our productive energy could be devoted to satisfying the needs of the mind and the spirit. The horse and buggy stage is far behind us. The railroad age, in relative terms at least, is rapidly vanishing, the plane has already moved into the jet era, and this in turn is being pushed by the rocket. In such a world there appear to be no limits to plausible flights of the imagination. It may therefore appear to be even somewhat pedestrian to suggest that perhaps half our productive energy could, before many decades are past, be devoted not to our physical needs, but to the intellectual, cultural, and recreational needs of modern urbanized communities.

So let us assume then, by way of illustration, that the publicly provided services constitute, say, one-half of the aggregate goods and services. I am not presenting any specific goal. I am discussing a tendency, a trend. And I am trying to think about the problem. It might be possible to place a price tag on a considerable fraction of these publicly provided services. This has the merit of expanding the role of the price system and lessening the role of taxes. Whether on balance this would be a good thing or a bad thing would have to be judged in each individual case. I do not like toll roads, but I would much rather have good toll roads than no roads at all. With respect to many goods and services a price tag helps to eliminate waste. If there is doubt, it might be well to lean toward the price-tag device, since this eases the problem of taxation and tends to enlarge the area within which incentives can operate.

Let us suppose then that of the 50 percentage points which I have assigned in our illustration to publicly provided services, 10 are amenable to the price-tag method. This would leave 40 per cent of the aggregate of all goods and services (public and private) to be financed from taxes. Possibly 5 per cent could be covered by the property tax, though many would like to reduce or even eliminate this tax. Could income taxes alone be pushed to a point sufficiently high to cover the remaining 35 per cent? Experience up to date suggests, I believe, that this may not be feasible. So high a rate could seriously dampen incentives. The alternatives then would be to "hook on" to the price tags of privately provided goods and services that are already displayed in the market place. This is what the sales tax does. It is a parasite, so to speak. It thrives on the backs of the price tags already set by market forces. We could imagine, then, by way of illustration, that 10 percentage points are covered by the parasitic price-tag method, namely, the sales tax. This would leave 25 percentage points to be covered by the income tax. Currently in the United States, Federal, State, and local income taxes amount to 15.2 per cent of total national income, while sales taxes amount as yet to only 5.0 per cent.

I have been considering sales taxes and income taxes as means to pay for goods and services. Let us suppose that the cost of a given bundle of goods and services goes up. To cover this increased cost, additional sales taxes or income taxes are imposed. This is necessary because existing public services have increased in cost. Since the bundle of services has not increased, this obviously means in fact an increase in the cost of living, exactly as would be the case if the grocer had raised his food prices. In this case the increased sales or income taxes should logically be included in the consumer price index. Sales taxes are so included now, but income taxes are not.

But neither sales taxes nor income taxes should be included in the cost of living index if they are levied to pay for new or additional services. In this latter case aggregate consumption has increased, but there has been no increase in the cost of living of a given consumer's basket of goods and services. If I buy more food, the money so spent does not indicate an increase in the consumer price index. Similarly if I pay a sales tax for *new* or *additional* public services, the money so spent should not be included in the calculation of the consumer price index.

To the extent that it might be deemed desirable to cut back expenditures on extravagant or useless gadgets, the price-tag parasite, namely, the sales tax, has the special merit that it does just that and at the same time provides revenue for financing useful community services. The price-tag parasite should clearly not be attached to the necessities of life, such as food or children's clothing. The great merit of the wartime purchase tax in Great Britain, during and after the war, was that high purchase-tax rates applied to luxuries, with lower rates on semiluxuries, and still lower rates on necessities. State sales taxes in our own country typically apply a uniform rate on a wide range of commodities, though 11 of the 35 States that have State or local sales taxes[5] exempt food or other necessities. In an age of gadgetry, a concomitant of the opulent society, the sales tax can play the highly useful role of restraining wasteful consumption. This could eventually become nearly as important as the revenue-raising function itself.

Lest I be misunderstood, let me say emphatically that I regard the progressive individual income tax and the corporation income tax as the central core and main bulwark of our tax structure, and it must continue to remain so. Without an income tax, the distribution of income would rapidly become oppressively concentrated. An income tax is essential for the preservation of a democratic society. Nevertheless, we shall be compelled, I believe, as the demand for public services grows, to supplement the income tax with sales taxes.

[5] Sometimes the sales taxes are levied by cities or counties.

State Finances in Trouble

The income tax, individual and corporate, is, and should remain, the chief source of revenue for the Federal government. Many of our more important States have no income tax. Still, all told, thirty-four States in the American Union have some form of income tax, usually progressive, with upper-limit marginal rates ranging from 3½ per cent to 11 per cent. The modal upper-limit marginal rates run from 5 to 7½ per cent. Alaska simply applies a State tax liability based on the returns of the Federal income tax. This method of assessing State income taxes has very much to commend it. It eliminates altogether the difficult and often confusing task of preparing two tax returns with different definitions of income, different rates, and different exemptions and deductions.

In recent years we have been drifting into the sales-tax method more and more at the State level. The choice has indeed not been altogether a free one. The issue is not being decided on its merits. We are drifting into it in large part because State politics in a large number of States has become stalemated at dead center. What is the reason? It is essentially this. We do not have majority rule in many of our State legislatures. The rural counties and the small towns often control. Large cities like New York, Los Angeles, Philadelphia, Chicago, Boston, Atlanta, and Providence are grossly underrepresented. In some cases a large city has no larger representation in the State senate than any small rural town. Overrepresentation of the rural areas continues to prevail in many States that have not changed their district representation for more than half a century.

Take Michigan. The governor was elected by majority vote. He wanted an income tax. Michigan has none. The

Senate, dominated by overrepresented rural towns, wanted to increase the 3 per cent sales tax. The governor represented the urban-liberal vote; the Senate represented rural-conservative opinion. Neither side would give in. The State was starved for funds to carry on even minimal functions. The conservatives won for the time being. A use tax of 1 per cent was added to the sales tax, the use-tax device being a subterfuge to avoid constitutional limitations. On October 26, 1959, the use tax was declared unconstitutional by the Michigan Supreme Court. This left the State with $80 million in arrears on bills and obligations long overdue, with a possible total arrears of $200 million by the end of the fiscal year. Makeshifts were invented to close the gap. But the battle is far from being over.

On balance, the large cities are progressive in their political thinking. The metropolitan areas already include more than 60 per cent of the total United States population and this majority is rapidly growing. Cities are mushrooming. The problems of urban living are not being met. They are piling up. And all the while, automation is narrowing the scope for employment in the material-goods sector. We are driven increasingly into the area of community services at a time when the political forces deny the rapidly growing urban population even the conventional types of community services. This is a dangerous situation. In earlier times it would have led to a social explosion, to riots, to the use of force, but today street barricades are not possible. Yet there appears to be no legal remedy. Everywhere we are searching for a way out of this impasse.

There is another reason why the States are waterlogged in a morass. States are afraid of levying taxes adequate to provide the services so urgently needed. They are afraid of interstate competition. A State income tax might drive industry into some other State. States compete in niggardliness.

Most of our largest industrial States have no income tax, and the reason is that they fear a competitive business disadvantage in relation to other States. Thus Illinois, Michigan, New Jersey, Ohio, Connecticut, Indiana, Pennsylvania, West Virginia, Rhode Island, Texas, Washington, and Florida have no State income tax. Even so progressive a governor as Ribicoff of Connecticut plays up the fact that Connecticut has no income tax in an effort to induce industry to locate in his State. In Germany it was always traditional for burgomasters to compete in the building and development of beautiful cities. In our country the tax competition between States works the other way. It has a depressing effect on good government. The result inevitably is that community services are starved.

Thus rural conservatism, which dominates the State legislatures, is bolstered up by the unhappy fact (which even progressively minded citizens cannot wholly ignore) that each State is fearful of losing its industries if taxes are raised. Every State is caught up in this snarl from which no one State can wholly extricate itself. Rural minorities with no conception of modern urban problems are in the saddle, and one factor that helps to keep them there is the scramble between States to attract new industries.

Breaking the Log Jam

We are in an impasse because we are afraid to use the only instrument that can break the log jam. And that is the Federal government. The "States' rights doctrine" is again in command. There has been talk in high places about goals for the future of America. But there is no program because the current philosophy is to let the States and local governments do the job.

Our metropolitan communities are bursting at the seams.

In fifteen years the population of our standard metropolitan areas will have increased by nearly 60 million people, bringing the total metropolitan population up to 160 million. This flood must inevitably sooner or later break the log jam. Minorities can dam up progress for a time, but not forever. The urban population is rapidly swelling into an overpowering majority. But what can the majority do, in view of the rural overrepresentation in the States? There is but one answer. The majority in the nation as a whole, the overwhelming urban majority will be compelled to employ the one powerful instrument at their command, namely the Federal government. By means of grants-in-aid and matching grants, the Federal government can introduce a counterbalancing kind of competition as an offset to the current downgrading competition between the states. States that refuse to match the grants-in-aid would be at a competitive disadvantage as compared with other States. This has been the answer in all federal governments—Australia, Canada, and Germany, and even to a degree in our own country. More recently, however, the Federal purse strings have been tightened. Just at the time when the wave of urbanism is reaching a crest, the States' rights dogma is being preached with renewed vigor.

But change is the law of life. The Federal government will once again, as in the great days of Hamilton and Marshall, become the instrument of progress. The Federal government is not, as some would have us believe, a foreign enemy. It is the one instrument by which the nation as a whole can overcome the local roadblocks to progress. It is the instrument of the majority. The States as now constituted are too often instruments of minorities, and they harbor within themselves the innumerable conflicts of an archaic system of overlapping jurisdictions.

On the other hand, however, let us give credit to the

extent that credit is due. I do not wish to exaggerate. Considering the difficulties under which the State and local governments operate, one cannot help but wonder that they have done as well as they have. It is a notable fact that State and local expenditures, exclusive of Federal grants-in-aid, represented virtually the same percentage of a rapidly rising national income in 1957 as in 1940–1941 and slightly higher than in 1929. In the meantime, however, the Federal expenditures (defense excluded) in relation to national income has increased 2.5 times. State and local expenditures, though in the same ratio as decades past, have not adequately kept pace with the demands of an advancing civilization. Still an absolute increase in State and local expenditures from $8.3 billion in 1940–1941 to $34.9 billion in 1957 discloses a capacity to raise revenue which must be regarded as remarkable when one keeps in mind the barriers to which I have referred. Omitting defense, State and local expenditures are indeed today of the same magnitude as Federal expenditures. State and local governments will continue (about this there can be no doubt) to play a major role in the Dual Economy. With appropriate Federal aid they can play an increasing role in the growing field of administration.

Indeed some hold the view that the record is so good that Federal aid is no longer necessary. It is sometimes argued that the national taxpaying capacity originates in the States, that the fiscal capacity of the Federal government derives from the States. Federal aid, it is said, means sending money to Washington and routing it back again with all the waste effort that that implies.

This argument is persuasive with many people, but it is wholly false. The American Union was formed in 1787 largely because the fiscal capacity of the separate States, loosely associated in the Confederation, was found to be utterly inadequate. The credit standing of the new national government was enormously greater than that of the original States combined. Indeed under Hamilton's leadership the national government undertook to assume the debt obligations of the States.

The national government is the only governmental unit that encompasses the entire national economy. Our great corporations draw their incomes from all parts of the country. But most of the large stockholders in these corporations reside in large, rich cities like New York. Only a national income tax can distribute the tax revenues back to the geographical areas from which the income flows are drawn. The same situation obtains between the States and their local communities, and this is the basic reason for State aid. Governmental subdivisions are not matched by corresponding subdivisions of the economy. Industry and business are national in scope. No governmental division can match this integrated whole except the Federal government.

Moreover, it must never be forgotten that the Federal government has access, as no State does, to the vast credit-creating powers of the central banking system—the Federal Reserve System. The Federal government can employ Federal Reserve credit resources to combat recessions and to foster growth. The financial capacity of the Federal government in a scale undreamed of in earlier periods was displayed in the First and the Second World Wars. The States together could have performed no such miracle of finance.

No one seriously questions this fact. Yet no inconsiderable amount of money is spent to make the general public think otherwise. The aim is to reduce or at least restrict Federal aid. The trend, however, will be inexorably the other way. The public services which an advanced society will require cannot be financed adequately except by Federal aid or else by the increasing assumption by the Federal government of functions now performed by the States. Federal aid is to be preferred in so far as local administration can effectively be performed by State and local governments. The Federal government, in its fiscal capacity, towers like a giant among the States. The whole is vastly greater than the sum of the parts.

Within the setting of a vigorous and expanding Federal government, local government and voluntary community activity can flourish. Many community projects can be undertaken by voluntary action. This has notably been demonstrated in the Scandinavian countries. Not only do they use government for the general welfare; they are also fertile in the development of free voluntary associations. A notable example is, of course, the great Danish cooperative societies which play such an enormous role—in many ways as important as the government itself. And in the field of health, while hospitals are owned and operated by the government (including county and municipal governments) and are virtually free to all citizens except for a nominal fee, voluntary associations also play a highly important role. Thus nearly all Danish citizens belong to health-insurance societies which provide full coverage to all members. A highly educated citizenry is capable not only of using the government as an instrument for the general welfare, but also of associating together in voluntary groups for the public good. Social institutions thereby escape from a rigid monolithic mold, and individual and group action is permitted to express itself partly through the national government, partly through local government, and partly through voluntary associations.

Our nineteenth-century tradition was for each individual to take care of himself. That was all very well in the days of an expanding frontier. But now we are crowding up in great metropolitan centers. Our community problems are hard upon us. The escapist effort—fleeing to the suburbs—only changes the locale of the problem. Individualist efforts —each family seeking to raise its own standard of living while neglecting the community problems of an ever-growing urbanism—can only end up in a deteriorating society. But despite opposition, we are nonetheless moving, though at an uneven pace, more and more toward the welfare state.

All modern free democracies are in fact Dual Economies— private ownership of the means of production with the government providing more and more community services. Private enterprise for the production of material goods; government (Federal, State, and local) playing the leading role in community programs—housing, health, hospitals, schools, urban transportation, programs for the aged, adult education, child-guidance clinics, recreational and cultural activities— in short, the many programs and activities that make for a truly civilized society.

PART III

Developed and Underdeveloped Countries

CHAPTER 9

THE UNITED STATES BALANCE OF PAYMENTS

The United States has made grants and loans for military and economic aid to foreign countries, amounting in the last dozen years or so to about $5 billion per annum. From July, 1945, to the end of 1959 the aggregate aid amounted to around $70 billion.[1]

Nothing of this sort has ever occurred before in all history. Still, let us beware of boasting. Five billion dollars per year is currently only 1 per cent of our Gross National Product. And except for the Marshall aid program, the bulk of the foreign aid has been military. Even now the economic aid is not more than ½ of 1 per cent of our GNP. Every year, *on the average*, our GNP rises by 3 per cent. Thus each annual *increase* in our GNP is six times our annual economic aid to foreign countries. Seen in this perspective it is evident that, in terms of sacrifice, our economic aid is relatively insignificant.

Dollar Shortage

Throughout most of this period the world was hungry for dollars. Our export of goods and services greatly ex-

[1] *Statistical Abstract of the United States*, 1959, p. 873 and supplementary estimates.

ceeded our imports. Our productive capacity had grown in rapid strides during and after the Second World War. In contrast the war had seriously crippled Europe. For some years the United States was the main source of supply. Europe notably was buying from us more than they were able to sell. They needed more dollars than they were earning. Hence the shortage of dollars. This gap in their balance of payments was filled by the grants and loans which the United States made available.

The United States was without a peer, economically speaking. We faced no strong competition. We alone, of the countries of the free world, had no balance-of-payments problem. The dollar was the strong currency throughout the world.

In Europe and elsewhere business firms wanted dollars in order to import needed raw materials and equipment, and individuals wanted dollars to buy durable consumers' goods and for travel abroad. Their governments could not allow unrestrained purchases because there were not enough dollars to go around. Foreigners, possessing ample funds in their own money, could not exchange their currency for dollars except in limited and closely controlled amounts. Their currency was not convertible into dollars.

As the years wore on, American business leaders and government officials were more and more urging Europeans to take measures to restore all-round convertibility of currencies. As European countries recovered, they were increasingly able to supply their own needs and even to increase their exports. The foreign demand for and the supply of dollars available to foreigners were gradually approaching a balance. There was a widespread demand for convertibility.

Convertibility

At long last in December, 1958, fairly full convertibility was restored. What was the reaction? Was everyone happy? Not at all. It is all rather ludicrous. No sooner was convertibility substantially restored than a great hue and cry was heard in this country about the precarious position of the dollar. Fears were expressed that we would lose all our gold, that we would price ourselves out of world markets, that the dollar would collapse.

During the period of inconvertibility the dollar was in a perfectly safe, sheltered, monopoly position. It had no serious competitors. Convertibility, however, means that more than one contestant has entered the race. Convertibility means that international competition has been restored. When weak currencies grow stronger, strong currencies inevitably grow relatively weaker. It is like a seesaw—when one currency goes up, another must come down. International balance means that each currency must struggle to hold its own in the race.

As the European countries were regaining their competitive strength, they gradually, though intermittently, built up their international reserves—gold and dollar balances. No country could restore convertibility of its currency until it had accumulated a sufficient reserve of foreign-exchange holdings to meet short-run fluctuations in its balance of international payments. Thus inevitably as Europe was building up its reserves, as in 1950–1955 and again in 1958–1959, the United States was transferring gold and dollar assets to foreign countries. This should have been expected. Apparently, judging from the consternation this has evoked, we wanted both convertibility and a monopoly hold on international monetary reserves.

American gold holdings reached $24.6 billion in 1949. From this level it declined, with some ups and downs, to $19.5 in December, 1959—an aggregate decline of $5.1 billion. In the meantime the gold reserves of foreign central banks and governments (excluding Russia and her satellites) rose from $11.0 billion in December, 1952, to $18.8 in September, 1959. Thus by 1959 the gold holdings of the free world were approximately equally divided between the United States and the rest of the free world. In addition to their gold holdings, these foreign countries held $16.2 billion of short-term dollar assets—in other words, aggregate international monetary reserves of $35 billion.

It was the world-wide recession of 1958 that brought the dollar balance-of-payments problem to a climax. In 1958 we transferred around $3.4 billion of gold and dollars to foreign countries. Of gold alone we lost $2.3 billion. In 1959 we lost another billion of gold and transferred a total of over $4 billion of gold and dollar holdings.

We had taken in our stride, without serious concern or even much discussion, the average transfer per year of $1.5 billion of gold and dollars to foreign countries in the seven years from 1950 to 1956. In 1957 we bounced back and gained half a billion of gold and dollars from the outside world. This was a special case (partly related to the Suez crisis) and it made us unduly confident. Then came 1958 and 1959 and the huge deficits in our international payments, averaging for these two years from $3.5 to $4.0 billion per year.

Thus for the first time we have become aware of a real balance-of-payments problem. But there is no ground for panic. We should not forget that a deficit in our balance of payments means an increase in aggregate monetary reserves. A moderate increase in foreign holdings of dollar balances is quite in order.

Distribution of International Reserves

The United States has quite properly lost its overwhelmingly preponderant position. And we can well afford to lose still more. A wide distribution of international reserves is absolutely essential in order to achieve viable convertibility.

During most of the postwar years, the gap which foreign countries suffered in their trade and service balance with the United States was more than filled by the vast grants and loans which we made to the outside world. Accordingly, the holdings by foreign countries of gold and dollar balances were rising until by September, 1959, they amounted to $35 billion.

But the distribution of international reserves has been unequal. West Germany has been absorbing an excess of international reserves, the net accumulation amounting to around $6.5 billion. In other words Germany, unlike the United States, has not been balancing her international accounts by loans and grants. This is the kind of thing Secretary Anderson had in mind when he said, quite rightly, that the time has come when other countries must participate in international lending. Substantial international payments surpluses need to be offset by long-term financing. Any country that permits its net exports to exceed its long-term financing is encroaching upon international reserves and creating an unbalance. Whenever any country fails to provide financing for its net exports whether by private capital outflow or by government loans and grants, such a country will necessarily be absorbing too large a part of the aggregate available supply of foreign exchange. Any large excess of net exports over the outflow of capital, says the Secretary, does not represent a satisfactory pattern of world payments.[2]

[2] *Monthly Review,* New York Federal Reserve Bank, October, 1959.

Here the Secretary is on thoroughly sound ground. He is also on sound ground when he insists that since many foreign countries have by now reached a sufficiently strong position to make their currency convertible, there is no longer any excuse for continued trade restrictions that discriminate against United States exports. These discriminations should speedily be removed. And world opinion, as recently voiced by the International Monetary Fund, agrees.

Tied Loans

Secretary Anderson has gone a step farther. On October 19, 1959, the managing director of the Development Loan Fund[3] said that in the future American loans to underdeveloped countries must normally be used to purchase goods in the United States. This represents, it is said, a sharp reversal of United States policy away from the liberal tradition so firmly advocated by Secretary Hull twenty-five years ago, when the Reciprocal Trade Agreements program was first inaugurated. Except for the Export-Import Bank, which was set up deliberately to increase United States exports and which has always made "tied loans," our policy has been not to attach strings to foreign-aid programs.

In appraising Secretary Anderson's proposal, however, it must be remembered that our foreign-aid loans to underdeveloped countries are not strictly business or bankable loans. They are soft loans repayable in the local currency of the borrowing country or easy-term loans made at subsidized rates of interest and with easy payment terms spread out

[3] The Development Loan Fund was established in 1957. It was designed to make so-called "soft loans" to underdeveloped countries—loans that do not measure up to banking standards and which are payable in the local currency of the borrowing country.

over many years. When the borrowing country buys equipment, for example, it is not merely the price that counts; it is also the terms of payment. The deal is a package deal—partly price and partly finance. Secretary Anderson's proposal, whatever its demerits may be, is not, strictly speaking, a violation of liberal trade or multiliberal trade principles. Any competing country is invited, indeed urged, to outbid the United States on the package deal. Terms of financing are no less important than price. If the loan were strictly a bankable loan, that would be another matter. But a soft loan or easy-term loan is in fact a subsidized loan.

Tied foreign-aid loans, I submit, cannot be put in the same category as free-market loans and cannot be judged in terms of multiliberal trade principles. Still, as an aid to multilateral trade and as an inducement to other countries to join us in the financing of foreign aid, we might well adopt a matching system. Using the "carrot on the stick" inducement device, we could agree that American loan funds might be used by any underdeveloped country prepared to match our loan offer on a fifty-fifty basis in order to purchase the equipment needed for its development. If no advanced country were willing to meet this offer, then the equipment would have to be purchased in the United States. If, however, some country—Germany, for example—were willing to supply half of the loan funds on as favorable terms as those offered by the United States, then all the equipment could, if so desired, be purchased in Germany. Such a program would constitute a challenge to other advanced countries to join with the United States in the provision of foreign aid. If successful it would make our foreign-aid program go twice as far.

I should myself feel much happier if our foreign-aid program were made in the form of grants instead of on a loan basis. What is urgently needed is a new Marshall aid program for the underdeveloped world. Is it not a strange thing that we made grants to the rich countries of Western Europe and loans to the poor countries? It does not make sense, and in fact I think we are fooling ourselves and the world if we think that these loans are really going to be repaid. Indeed the soft loans (namely, the loans repayable in the currency of the borrowing country) tend in the very nature of the case to become disguised grants. And the easy long-term loans, theoretically repayable in dollars, can easily under the pressure of balance-of-payments difficulties become in effect involuntary grants. We have had experience with that sort of thing before. Witness the First World War loans. The whole thing simply became unworkable.

Viewed in terms of practical politics, it is of course not difficult to see that the aid to underdeveloped countries presents no such urgency, in terms of our own national security, as did the Marshall aid program. But in terms of economics the case is the same for both. Still if grants are politically impossible, loans are far better than nothing. The problems of repayment will have to be dealt with in the future.

Our Gold-reserve Problem

As to our own balance-of-payments problem, we shall have to learn how to stand up in world competition. We could, however, do some things to help protect our net international reserve position. For one thing we could free the $12 billion or so of gold which is now held as a reserve against the note and deposit liabilities of the Federal Reserve banks. This $12 billion of gold is currently completely immobilized by reason of the legal requirement which compels the Federal Reserve banks to maintain 25 per cent gold reserve against their note and deposit liabilities. This reserve requirement serves no useful purpose,[4] and all this gold could just as well be set free for international payment. In addition we could pretty effectively stop any speculative drain on our gold supply by giving a firm exchange guarantee in terms of gold to all foreign governments and central-bank holders of dollar balances. This would allay any fears that such holders might otherwise have of losses entailed by reason of possible future increases in the dollar price of gold. Such a guarantee is not without precedent. Under Article II of the European Monetary Agreement, holders of sterling balances enjoy a firm exchange guarantee in terms of the United States dollar. Accordingly "European Central banks are now free to accumulate sterling, if they so choose, without taking any exchange risk in the case of a devaluation of sterling with respect to the dollar."[5] A similar guarantee of dollars with respect to gold would remove any incentive on the part of gold speculators to transfer dollars into gold in anticipation of a possible future devaluation of the dollar.

In the event that these reforms were adopted, the continued accumulation of short-term dollar holdings by foreign countries need be no cause for alarm. In an expanding world market foreign countries will need a growing volume of dollar assets. Should these holdings of dollar balances accumulate beyond the level desired for purposes of international liquidity, we may be sure that they could advantageously be employed to purchase American securities and real estate. The United States offers highly profitable financial investment opportunities for funds accumulating in excess of the

[4] See the excellent statement by Dr. Roy L. Reierson, Vice President and chief economist of the Bankers Trust Company, New York, in the *New York Times*, November 19, 1959.

[5] Robert Triffin, "The Return to Convertibility," *Banca Nazionale del Lavoro Quarterly Review*, no. 48, March, 1959, p. 46.

requirements of liquidity. Already in 1959 a substantial development along this line was under way. Foreign purchases of American stocks, bonds, and other long-term investments amounted to more than half a billion dollars. We can therefore expect that, should the currents of world trade tend in the decade ahead to create a "glut of dollars," foreign investments in the United States will grow. In this manner, an "unfavorable balance of trade," so-called, would be offset by a net inflow of capital into the United States.

It could be argued that the net flow of capital will tend to move in the opposite direction by reason of investment by American concerns in branch factories abroad. This could indeed for a while intensify our balance-of-payments problem. But an imbalance of this sort soon tends to cure itself because of the increasing back-flow of earnings from such investments. The repatriated earnings had already reached $2.6 billion in 1958, and they are steadily climbing. They are indeed already roughly equal to current annual net private investments abroad. So the one offsets the other.

One final word about the willingness of foreigners to hold dollar balances and the fear that there may develop a serious "run on gold." It should be borne in mind that the whole picture with respect to such international runs has changed since the dreadful days of the thirties. We now have the International Monetary Fund through which consultations between governments and central banks go on almost continuously. There is a degree of cooperation and a sense of international responsibility such as was not present in the thirties. On this point Allan Sproul has made a highly relevant statement. He says that "only official foreign holders of United States assets can convert them directly into gold, and it is these official holders, of course, who should be aware of common international responsibilities for the effective working of the existing international gold exchange standard, which rests so heavily on the continued strength and stability of the dollar." [6]

In a growing market international monetary reserves must also grow. True, the accumulation of reserves does not *cure* balance-of-payments problems. Large reserves do, however, enable a country to take a deliberate view of the problem. Ample reserves can tide over temporary difficulties and forestall hasty and unwarranted drastic action. Currency depreciation or exchange control may indeed become necessary if a *fundamental* disequilibrium has developed. But if a country's international reserves are inadequate, it may be pushed into taking steps that are not called for.

International monetary reserves can, and are, being increased from three sources: (1) gold production, (2) increases in liquid holdings of key currencies (dollars and sterling, but especially dollars), and (3) increases in the lending resources of the International Monetary Fund. Those who deprecate the growth of dollar holdings by foreign central banks and governments lose sight of the fact that this is, under current conditions, a much-needed source of additional international reserves. And there is no evidence thus far that foreign countries prize gold more highly than dollars. From 1954 to 1959 the gold holdings of foreign countries increased $5.3 billion (of which only $2.2 billion came from United States gold hoards), but dollar balances increased even more —$5.8 billion. Had gold been prized above dollars, dollar balances would have increased less than gold holdings.

The three methods outlined above are actually now in operation as means to increase international monetary reserves. Some economists feel that currently available methods are not adequate. Sir Roy Harrod wishes to increase the price of gold, and Professor Robert Triffin advocates con-

[6] See *National Objectives and the Balance of Payments Problem*, Committee for Economic Development, February, 1960, p. 7.

verting the International Monetary Fund into a truly central bank. Triffin's proposal is similar to the much-discussed Clearing Union that was advocated by Keynes nearly twenty years ago, but was set aside at Bretton Woods in favor of the International Monetary Fund scheme. Under Triffin's plan an International Central Bank would have the power to create international reserve balances which, in addition to gold holdings, would become the sole means of international payment. Key currencies would no longer be held as monetary reserves. The International Bank would create central-bank credit (reserve balances) against assets or claims acquired from the borrowing country exactly in the manner that the Federal Reserve System creates member-bank balances in favor of such commercial banks as wish to borrow from the System.

Both the Harrod and the Triffin proposals appear currently to be outside the pale of practical politics. For the time being, we shall probably have to look to gold production, increases in dollar holdings, and increases in the resources of the International Monetary Fund for the needed growth in international monetary reserves.

Mass Markets and Technical Progress in Europe

Is the United States losing out in world markets? Are we pricing ourselves out of the market? Is the dollar becoming a soft currency?

The *Economic Report of the President* of January, 1960, in the section dealing with this problem, shows, I think, quite clearly that there is no ground for taking an alarmist view. Nonetheless, it may well be that we are just now entering upon a quite new phase in our trade relations with Western Europe. Until now it has been customary to refer to the "dollar shortage" problem. We were always outselling our competitors. In my opinion the most persuasive explanation for this state of affairs is the view effectively presented by my colleague John Williams, namely, that the United States was always one step ahead of Europe in terms of an advancing technology. The result was that we were always able, with our mass-production technique, to capture world markets, particularly in the fields of consumer durables, machinery, chemicals, etc. It is not impossible that we may now be losing this advantage.

And the reason is not something that is happening to us. The reason is rather to be sought in changes going on in Europe. Western Europe is just now emerging above the threshold that separates small, local markets from mass markets. Incomes in Western Europe have at long last reached a level high enough to open mass-production markets for automobiles, household electrical appliances, and consumers' durables in general. And all this is being aided by the impending union of the "six countries" into a common market area. Mass production in a huge tariff-free market buoyed up by rising living standards—this is the basis for the technical revolution already visible over the horizon in Western Europe. This development will inevitably narrow, and in time perhaps eliminate altogether, the agelong productivity differential between the United States and Europe.

Such a development could put a severe squeeze on the United States balance of payments. It can, however, be expected that this squeeze will progressively be softened by a strong upward pressure of wage rates in Europe. As the productivity differential between Western Europe and the United States disappears, so also will the wage differential. The development of mass markets and mass-production techniques in Europe is precisely the leverage needed to lift European living standards to the level obtaining in the United States.

CHAPTER 10

UNITED STATES RECESSIONS

At long last the United States is confronted, as we have seen in the previous chapter, with the problem of managing its balance of payments. All countries, in a changing and competitive world, must face up to this problem just as they must also face up to the problems of stability and growth. There is, however, an important difference between the developed and the underdeveloped countries. The developed countries are in a far more favorable position to influence their international-payments position by voluntary action on their own part. The underdeveloped countries are often swept by world forces too powerful for them to counteract. The underdeveloped countries are not infrequently at the mercy of policies dictated by the advanced countries or at least by forces emanating from the advanced countries.

World-wide Impact of Recessions

The most obvious example is the powerful impulse that spreads to the underdeveloped countries in periods of recession or depression in the advanced countries. A recession in an advanced country means indeed unemployment and a slowing down, or even decline in economic growth. But it also tends to improve its balance-of-payments position. Inflationary pressures are reduced, imports tend to fall off, and raw-material prices decline. This helps the advanced country with respect to its balance-of-payments position, but it hits the primary producing country.

This is exactly what happened in 1958. Indeed it may be said that the return to convertibility of the European currencies in late 1958 was achieved at no mean cost to the underdeveloped countries. Not only was the external position of the European countries very favorably affected by the fall in the prices of imported raw materials, but in addition, the poor countries of the world tended to keep up their purchases from the advanced countries by running down their exchange reserves. Thus while the advanced countries gained, the underdeveloped countries lost.

The 1958 episode can be regarded, more or less, as a standard model—a model which fits pretty well the countries of Western Europe on the one side and the Asiatic countries and Latin America on the other side. The United States, however, is a sort of hybrid. The United States is at the same time one of the largest exporters of raw materials and also one of the largest exporters of finished goods. It is also a heavy importer of both raw materials and finished goods. Accordingly the impact of a world-wide recession on the United States balance-of-payments position is problematical, depending upon the relative weight of different factors.

The recession of 1958 hit the underdeveloped countries hard, while it was easy in its impact on the advanced countries of Western Europe. The reason is this. It involved a decline in the purchases of raw materials, both agricultural and mineral, by advanced countries. The terms of trade of the underdeveloped countries was seriously affected. The recession was world-wide. In Europe no less than in the United States there was a fairly sharp decline in investment in fixed capital and in inventories. But the 1958 recession in the United States involved scarcely any decline in personal income and no decline at all in consumption expenditures. Since consumption did not fall off, imports into the United States from Europe were very well maintained. The recession in Europe, however, cut down on European purchases of American raw materials. And so the balance-of-payments deficit in the United States sharply increased. In Europe, however, a surplus in their balance of payments developed, since raw-material prices fell and exports to America were well maintained.

The 1958 business recession, though unusual in various ways, was typical in the sense that there was a fairly sharp decline of investment both in inventories and in fixed capital outlays. In a recession of this type it can usually be expected that Europe will increase its holdings of international monetary reserves, while the United States, and especially the underdeveloped countries, will suffer a decline in reserves. Underdeveloped countries suffered in terms of balance of payments and also in a heavy decline in national income owing to the drop in the value of exports. A recession both in the United States and in Europe, though relatively mild, will typically cause serious suffering and hardship in the underdeveloped countries. Indeed in the 1958 recession the losses sustained by the underdeveloped countries by reason of the decline in raw-material prices by far outweighed any foreign aid given over several years.

This underscores how important it is to prevent a recession in the advanced countries and particularly how important it is to prevent a sharp decline in investment in fixed capital, i.e., in the heavy-goods industries. For such a decline means a sharp reduction in the imports of raw materials and consequently a serious loss of value of exports and of income in the underdeveloped countries. We do great damage to our foreign-aid program by permitting the continuation of these cyclical fluctuations.

A country like India, for example, with a population of 415 million people compared with our 180 million, has a Gross National Product of only $25 billion compared with our GNP of $500 billion. The 1958 recession brought a loss in GNP in real terms of $25 billion below the 1957 projected trend level[1] (account being taken here of the normal growth trend of 3 per cent per annum). Accordingly our recession *loss* was just equal to the *entire* annual GNP in India. A small percentage decline in our GNP can cause a sharp decline percentagewise in the aggregate value of exports in an under-developed country. Magnitudes that seem small to us loom large in countries where GNP is so incredibly small as, for example, that of India.

The Cycle Is Still with Us

Three recessions within the last twelve years underscore the fact that the cycle is still with us. Distinguished economists, notably Cassel and Hawtrey, expressed the view after the First World War that the business cycle was a thing of the past. And similarly after the Second World War some economists thought that the concept of the cycle was obsolete and no longer applicable to present-day economic conditions. Huge government budgets, social security, the farm price-support program, the built-in stabilizers—all these, it was argued, now played so large a role that automatic market forces were no longer able to produce periodic fluctuations in output and employment.

[1] As I have noted elsewhere, the GNP in 1958 may well have been $35 billion below the potential growth line. We fell considerably below substantially full utilization of our productive resources in the preceding 1957 peak.

Experience has proved both of these postwar judgments to be wrong. True, after the First World War the first recession (1921), though sharp, was brief; and it was followed by the recessions of 1924 and 1927—both short and mild. But then came the terrible depression of the thirties, the worst in our entire history. And now after the Second World War we have had three minor recessions. There were those who feared that the third might have developed into a serious depression, but this did not happen, or perhaps in any case we would not have allowed it to happen.

The Essence of Cycle Movements

All these recessions, whether severe or mild, can be fitted without difficulty into the pattern of business-cycle theory. They were not sporadic or accidental. They were the result of well-known forces operating in a price economy which employs a large amount of fixed and working capital.

According to the investment-cycle theory, the business cycle is essentially a fluctuation in the output of investment goods. Investment goods consist of: (1) inventory stocks of raw, semifinished, or finished products held by manufacturers, wholesalers, and retailers and (2) fixed capital, namely, producers' equipment and new construction of all kinds, especially business plant and residential structures.

Inventory stocks comprised in 1957, for example, $180 billion. A net addition of a mere 5 per cent or a net reduction of 5 per cent in these stocks of goods would mean an increase or decrease in output of nearly $10 billion. Worse yet, if a net addition had been going on for a few years, until the stocks had been built up to current and anticipated sales requirements, the mere *cessation* of "stock piling" would cause a decline in output. And if the stocks were now actually drawn down, the aggregate decline in output could be very great. The mere *cessation of growth* produces a decline, and a drawing down of stocks intensifies the decline.

Inventory stocks are built up to meet anticipated increases in sales and sometimes to beat price increases. But continued accumulation of stocks is checked by limited warehouse space and by interest and other costs of carrying. So, every inventory-investment boom comes to an end. From peak to peak the period of oscillation is typically around three to four years.

An inventory recession may or may not be accompanied by a decline in the output of fixed capital goods—producers' equipment and new construction. When such a decline does occur, the recession is likely to become pretty severe unless vigorous steps are taken to offset it.

Recessions may also be caused by a drastic decline in government expenditures. Such a decline will tend to induce a decline in stock piling and in outlays on fixed capital, but it is of course always possible that other factors, such as new technological developments, might more or less offset this tendency.

New investment in fixed capital (i.e., an increase in the stock of producers' equipment, business plant, both commercial and industrial, railroads, public utilities, houses) is induced primarily by two powerful growth factors: (1) growth in population[2] and (2) technological developments. After some years of heavy investment overcapacity may develop and this can be the beginning of a severe slump.

[2] The increase in any one factor of production (e.g., labor) will cause an increase in demand (an upward shift in the productivity schedule) for the other factors. Thus an increase in labor will increase the demand for capital and so cause an increased flow of investment. Population growth therefore stimulates expansion where labor is relatively scarce.

The Built-in Stabilizers

For the most part, the postwar recessions were caused by factors not unlike those with which we had long been familiar in our prewar history. Each cycle is indeed different, but the basic underlying institutional factor—a price system operating with large stocks of fixed and working capital—is common to both prewar and postwar cycles. Nonetheless there is a difference between the postwar cycles and the cycles preceding the nineteen thirties. The postwar fluctuations have been tempered by two new stabilizing factors—products of the New Deal reforms and the Keynesian revolution in economic thinking and policy. They are (1) the built-in stabilizers and (2) a deliberate (though admittedly poorly executed) full-employment policy. In addition our enormous postwar government budgets (Federal, State, and local) have powerfully contributed to sustained full employment.[3]

The built-in stabilizers are cushions, tending to soften the downward cumulative process once recession has set in. They operate to sustain the disposable income of individuals and so to help maintain consumption expenditures. Old-age and unemployment-insurance payments, the farm price-support program, the decline both in corporate income taxes (as profits decline) and in personal income taxes, especially in a steeply progressive income tax structure—all these operate automatically as shock absorbers when investment (outlays on new capital goods) declines. In addition to these built-in stabilizers, deliberate policy has increasingly come to play a more important role. In the postwar period corporations have not only maintained dividends; they have increased them in each recession period. The government has, partly by acci-

[3] Federal, State, and local budgets combined amounted to $132 billion in 1959.

dent, and partly by design, followed more or less a counter-cyclical fiscal policy. This includes, among other things, tax cuts in recession periods, increased payments to veterans, supplementary unemployment-insurance benefits, Federal housing programs, and increased public works and military expenditures.

All three postwar recessions disclose the impressive role that the built-in stabilizers and deliberate countercyclical policy have played in maintaining disposable income despite the decline in GNP. Thus in the 1954 recession the gap between GNP and disposable income was narrowed by $17.2 billion from the peak quarter (second quarter of 1953) to the bottom quarter (third quarter of 1954). The $17.2 billion cut in the spread between GNP and disposable income was represented by a fall of $14.4 billion in GNP and a rise of $2.8 in disposable income. Similarly in the 1958 recession the gap between GNP and disposable income was narrowed by $14.7 billion from the peak quarter (third quarter of 1957) to the bottom quarter (first quarter of 1958). The decline of $16.8 billion in GNP operated, however, to narrow the gap between GNP and disposable income by only $14.7 billion, since the initial gap was augmented, in this case, by a moderate decline of $2.1 billion in disposable income.

These are quarterly data. Yearly data of course disclose much smaller fluctuations. Employing yearly data, we find that the gap between GNP and disposable income was cut by only $1.7 billion from 1948 to 1949, $6.7 billion from 1953 to 1954, and $9.4 billion from 1957 to 1958.

Differences between the Postwar Recessions

There are some striking differences between the three post-war recessions, both with respect to the factors that produced them, and the measures that were employed (1) to stop them before they developed into deep depressions and (2) to bring about a rapid recovery.

The 1949 recession was peculiarly an inventory recession. Not much more needs to be said. The shift in inventory accumulation involved not merely the heavy cessation of postwar stock piling, but this cessation moved rapidly on to a pretty drastic cutback in inventory stocks. The combined effect brought a decline of nearly $8 billion in inventory investment from 1948 to 1949.[4] This was reinforced by a moderate decline ($2.4 billion) in fixed capital investment. Taking the two together, the predominating factor in this recession was a $10 billion drop in investment outlay.

In contrast, the 1958 recession (the 1954 recession will be reviewed below) was both an "inventory recession" and a "fixed capital recession," the decline being nearly $6 billion in each category. This recession was moreover strongly weighted down by a cutback in net exports ($3.7 billion). It was a three-pronged recession, not simply an inventory recession. From the peak quarter in 1957 to the bottom quarter in 1958 the decline in gross private domestic investment was $17 billion.

There was another difference. The 1949 recession was accompanied by a fairly strong drop in prices. In contrast, the 1958 recession witnessed a moderate rise in prices—a rare occurrence in business-cycle history. It is possible that "power factors"—corporate administered prices and trade-union wage pressures—played a role here.

The Role of Government Expenditures

The automatic stabilizers played a large role in both cases. Moreover, in the 1949 recession the tax cut of 1948 helped

[4] I limit myself here to annual data. If quarterly data were used, the fluctuations would of course be greater from peak to trough.

to sustain private expenditures. In 1949, 1958, and 1959 government cash payments were boosted on a large scale, whether by design or accident—$8.0 billion from 1948 to 1949, $8.0 billion from 1957 to 1958, and $8.9 billion from 1958 to 1959.[5] This last point is especially noteworthy in view of the fact that it is often said that speedy and effective anti-cyclical action in terms of government expenditures is not possible, and so reliance must be placed primarily upon tax reduction and monetary ease. I have no quarrel with the tax reduction and monetary-ease methods, but I believe it to be highly important that we do not hastily jump at the conclusion that the expenditure method is impractical. Experience does not justify this view. Indeed in both the 1949 and the 1958 recessions, apart from the built-in stabilizers, it was the fairly sharp increases in government expenditures that stopped the downturn and aided recovery.

Consumption of Goods and Services Maintained

The combined effect of the stabilizers and increased government expenditures (and in 1949 the tax cut) prevented any fall in consumption; indeed it caused a rise in both the recessions of 1949 and of 1958. In real terms the increase was $5.5 billion in 1949 and $2.8 billion in 1958. The increase in consumption in real terms was aided in 1949 by the decline in consumer prices, but precisely the opposite was true of the 1958 recession. Here the rise in consumer prices, particularly of services, prevented any large rise in consumption in real terms.

In the 1958 recession the combined effect of the stabilizers, the deliberately increased transfer payments, and the increase

[5] *Economic Report of the President*, January, 1960, p. 216. Of the $8 billion, $5.7 billion was Federal, and of the $8.9, $6.6 billion was Federal.

in government purchases of goods and services—the combined effect of all these was not sufficient to offset the drastic decline in real terms of gross private investment (including net exports). The consumer plus government offset was only $6.8 in real terms against a $17.1 decline in gross investment, leaving a drop in real GNP of $10.3 billion. In the 1949 recession, on the other hand, the combined effect of the stabilizers, the deliberate increases in transfer payments, the tax cut of 1948, and increased government outlays produced a net increase in real terms of consumption and government outlays of $11.7 billion which balanced approximately the decline in investment.

How Then Did the Economy Suffer?

Just how then did the economy suffer from these two recessions (1949 and 1958)? Aggregate consumption in real terms, let it be noted, increased—$5.5 billion in 1949 and $2.8 billion in 1958. And the volume of government-purchased civilian goods and services in real terms also increased—$3.7 billion in 1949 and $5.1 billion in 1958. In what sense then did the economy suffer?

Consider the postwar record, year by year, of the social dividend. By "social dividend" I mean the aggregate flow, in real terms, of the goods and services purchased by individuals together with the *civilian* goods and services supplied by governments, Federal, State, and local. Now the amazing fact is that the social dividend, so defined, has grown every single year since the end of the Second World War, including the three recession years. True, the average increase in the three recession years was only $6.7 billion, while the average increase in the period 1948 to 1959 inclusive was $10.3 billion. The persistent rise each year, even in recession years, is, however, a significant new achievement.

But while the social dividend was persistently rising year by year, there occurred nevertheless fluctuations in output and employment. After subtracting the social dividend from the Gross National Product there remain three rather volatile components of the GNP; namely, (1) gross private investment, (2) net export-surplus, and (3) military expenditures. The first two, in particular, are highly volatile, and together they largely explain the fluctuations in output and employment, despite the persistent growth in the social dividend.

The economy as a whole suffered a decline in the net addition to its stock of capital goods. The decline in real terms was $11.7 billion in 1949 and $13.7 billion in 1958. From the peak quarter in 1957 to the bottom quarter in 1958 investment in real terms dropped $18.3 billion. This decline in capital outlays caused unemployment. Recession hits hard at certain points in the economy. It is the unemployed and the partially unemployed that bear the major brunt of recessions. The employment effect must be measured not merely in terms of the decline in employment, but also in terms of the inability of the system to absorb the new entrants to the labor market. This amounts to around 900,000 young people, who are peculiarly affected because they have not yet earned the right to unemployment insurance.

We have learned how to minimize the impact on the economy as a whole. The aggregative figures look pretty favorable—an aggregate increase in private consumption and in the public consumption of goods and services. General aggregate well-being is obviously going forward even in recession years. But even though unemployment hits a restricted segment of the community, the numbers involved are, even in mild recessions, by no means inconsequential. The aggregate unemployment was 3,682,000 in 1949 and 4,681,000 in 1958.[6] Including dependents, this makes an

[6] To this must be added involuntary *part-time* unemployment.

average aggregate population without *employment* means of support in these two recession years of 10,450,000 persons. Many were of course receiving unemployment compensation payments.

Recessions slow down growth. It is always a mistake to calculate the decline in output and in employment from the preceding peak. It should always be calculated from the growth trend line. Viewed in this way, each recession means a loss of GNP of $15 billion per year *greater than the figures usually quoted.*

The Special Case of the 1954 Recession

With respect to the primary causal factors involved, the special case of the 1954 recession remains to be considered. This recession was due almost entirely to the drop in governmental expenditures incident to the cessation of the Korean conflict. The decline in government outlays on goods and services in real terms amounted to $10.9 billion. There was indeed also a decline in investment in inventories of $3 billion in real terms. Inventories thus played a role, either primary or secondary, in each of the three postwar recessions. In the 1954 recession net exports in real terms increased by nearly $2 billion, and fixed capital outlays rose by half a billion.

How then did the over-all economy fare in the 1954 recession? Consumption in real terms increased by $3.3 billion. Capital investment (fixed and inventory) decreased by $2.5 billion. The goods and services consumed by government decreased by nearly $11 billion. Unemployment increased by 1,700,000, bringing total unemployment up to 3,578,000.

The decline in government purchases of goods and services was not, however, in the area of civilian expenditures. The decline was in military hardware and in the costs of actual military operations in the field. Private consumption increased moderately, private investment declined a little, but not enough to register any very adverse effect. But hardship was concentrated, as in all recessions, upon a certain group—the unemployed and their families. And aggregate private consumption and investment was slowing down in growth—a failure to keep up with the rising trend.

Apart from the built-in stabilizers the most important anticyclical weapon employed in the 1954 recession was the large $7 billion repeal of some considerable part of the tax increases due to the Korean conflict, along with the dramatic changeover to monetary ease by the Federal Reserve in the spring of 1953. Further, the 1954 tax law offered a stimulus to recovery in the provision for accelerated depreciation. Down payments and amortization schedules were placed on easier terms. Installment credit jumped from $23.6 billion to $29.0 billion from 1954 to 1955, while mortgage debt increased from $105.4 billion to $120.9 billion. Out of all this developed an unhealthy spurt in investment in producers' plant and equipment, resulting in excess capacity and finally, in the latter half of 1957, a fairly sharp drop in investment outlays.

To sum up, over and above the automatic cushioning effect of the built-in stabilizers, the major anticyclical weapon employed in the 1949 and 1958 recessions was a substantial increase in government expenditures. In the 1954 recession the major weapon employed was a sharp reduction in tax rates.

Apart from the effect of *countercyclical* fiscal operations, note should also be taken of the stabilizing impact of *aggregate* governmental budgets, Federal, State, and local. While investment is an unruly and highly volatile component of the GNP, government expenditures have proved to be highly stable on an upward trend. The stable component (government expenditures) has spectacularly outdistanced the unruly component (investment) during the last thirty years. Thus government budgets (Federal, State, and local) in 1929 amounted to only $10 billion compared with $16 billion for gross private investment in a GNP of $100 billion, while in 1959 the aggregate governmental budgets amounted to $132 billion compared with only $70 billion of gross private investment outlays in a GNP of $480 billion.

What Must We Do to Stabilize the Cycle?

I have already discussed, at various points in the preceding chapters, what needs to be done if we are to make further progress in subduing the cycle. I shall very briefly summarize them here.

We should strengthen our built-in stabilizers in two ways. First we should introduce a system of automatic adjustment of tax rates. *Basic* tax rates should be fixed by Congress and changed from time to time according to the requirements of a balanced economy. In the usual case these would be the prevailing rates. Employment and industrial output should be permitted to fluctuate within a certain range along a rising trend without any automatic tax-rate adjustment. But whenever employment and industrial output fall below the designated range, tax rates should automatically be reduced in accordance with a prearranged schedule which had already been acted upon by the Congress. And if the employment and industrial output rose above the designated range of permissible fluctuations from the trend, then the tax rates should automatically be raised according to the prearranged schedule.

It may well be that other criteria, besides employment and the industrial production index, should be given a certain weight in the automatic adjustment schedule. And it is possible that the President should be authorized to veto the rate adjustment which otherwise would automatically go into effect. He should be required, however, in the event that such a step were taken, to make a report to Congress stating the grounds of his veto.

In the second place, the built-in stabilizers could be substantially strengthened by the enactment of a Federal Supplementary Unemployment Insurance Law. The present system of unemployment insurance administered by the States would continue undisturbed. But whenever unemployment rose above a designated trend level, Federal insurance would come into force supplementing the present State system.

Under this scheme the State system would become primarily a means of ensuring against seasonal unemployment, while the Federal system would become the principal means of ensuring against cyclical unemployment. To strengthen the anticyclical built-in stabilizers and to redress the grievous injustice of society loading the losses of recessions onto the backs of those who, in consequence of cyclical instability, lose their jobs through no fault of their own, the Federal unemployment insurance should be far more generous than any of the State systems now in operation. I suggest that the Federal system should ensure payments to an unemployed person equal to three-fourths of his average weekly wage. As soon as the Federal supplements became payable, the State payments would cease altogether. The State system could then concentrate on seasonal unemployment and the milder cyclical savings. This would enable the States to put their systems on a stronger financial basis and enable them to raise their payments. Indeed *minimum* State standards should be fixed by Federal legislation.

In the third place, the system of built-in stabilizers could be strengthened by introducing a system of countercyclical adjustment of accelerated depreciation. I shall not repeat here what I have already said above. See in this connection Chapter 4 in this book.

Finally, we need still stronger means than those so far

employed to choke off excessive investment booms. Monetary policy, interest-rate adjustment, and Federal Reserve action to limit the availability of credit are the primary means now employed to achieve this goal. If any reader should at first feel a bit shocked at the idea of choking off excessive investment, he should recall to mind the fact that this is exactly what monetary policy aims to do. Those who ardently advocate monetary restraint should not find it too difficult to support a tax designed to restrain investment. Again, there is no need to reiterate the argument in favor of such a tax. I have discussed this matter in Chapter 4 in this book.

Conclusion: Growth, Price Stability, and World-wide Equilibrium

In conclusion, it should be noted that a closer control of the cycle is imperative if we are to make headway on both the problem of growth and the problem of price stability. As long as the cycle is allowed to develop excessive investment booms, the ratchet price trend effect is likely to continue on into the future. And as long as we permit these *spurts* of price inflation, we are likely to be so concerned about the inflation problem that we will not dare to push on toward full employment.

As long as we permit fluctuations of even such relatively small magnitudes as those of 1949, 1954, and 1958, we shall continue to fall short of the goals we strive for with respect to both growth and price stability. Even more important possibly, from the standpoint of world-wide economic equilibrium and indeed world peace, is the impact of these recessions upon the underdeveloped countries. We help them with foreign-aid programs on the one hand, and we do them severe damage, on the other hand, with our periodic recessions.

CHAPTER II

ECONOMIC DEVELOPMENT: THE CASE OF INDIA

Of all the underdeveloped countries not yet drawn into the Soviet orbit, India is by far the largest and most important. And it is the one with which I myself am most familiar, having spent eight months in the academic year 1957–1958, under Yale University and Ford Foundation auspices, as guest professor at the University of Bombay.

In thinking about the problems of India, I find it useful to think of her as two countries—"Urban India" and "Rural India." Let us suppose that Urban India, including all the more important commercial and industrial sections, comprises one nation with a population of around 60 million. Urban India so constituted would include all the great metropolitan centers together with the larger and middle-sized cities. These urban centers are in fact knit together by a network of communications—a highly developed railway system and a modern and up-to-date airplane service. Business leaders in urban centers are in close contact. Many Indians spend their entire lives in an urban community and so are hardly aware of the existence of the vast rural sector. I have met urbanites in Bombay who insist that they have never visited a rural Indian village.

Urban India

Urban India, though it comprises less than 15 per cent of the entire Indian population, is the sector that counts. It contains the 3 to 4 million (less than 1 per cent of the population) that speak English. From this group come the leaders in politics and business—the great banks, the shipping companies, trading companies, manufacturing companies, the great textile industry, the iron and steel industry, the leading commercial and industrial concerns. The great cities have urban transit systems, more or less like those of any European or American city. There are office buildings, banks, hotels, apartment houses. There are fine residential areas with spacious lawns. There are often large playing fields and parks, especially in such important centers as Bombay, Madras, Calcutta, and New Delhi. There are elegant racing courses and clubhouses. And at certain hours of the day some streets may be congested with automobile traffic. Every city is well-supplied with newspapers, both in English and in the native languages. The English newspapers are excellent, often superior to the usual run of American newspapers—excluding from this comparison the half dozen or so of our really first-class papers. There are good bookstores and a wide range of cultural activities. There are some thirty large universities. Associated with these universities are hundreds of colleges. There is a growing number of technical schools—engineering, medicine, and commerce. In each of the great cities there is a large circle of highly educated persons. Mingled with the educated native population is a considerable number of resident foreigners engaged in commerce, industry, or finance. During a recent visit to India Prime Minister Macmillan said that there are more British businessmen in India today than at the end of the British rule more than a decade ago.

Such a country can scarcely be called an underdeveloped country. Urban India could better be described as a semideveloped country.

Like all semideveloped countries, Urban India has its seamy side—slums, filth, congestion, poverty. Streets everywhere teem with thousands upon thousands of people miserably clothed and suffering from disease and malnourishment. Huddled together in stifling tenement quarters, many prefer to sleep on the sidewalks and thousands are simply "pavement dwellers." It is estimated that 250,000 people sleep on the pavements every night in the city of Bombay. One sees them everywhere, even in the better districts. There are thousands of beggars, many of them professionals who ply begging as a trade. Small businesses like shoe repairing and hairdressing are conducted right on the pavement. Humans are used as draft animals in competition with scrawny and ill-fed bullocks. On the outskirts of large cities are whole colonies of miserable huts that display a depth of poverty which cannot be described by words. One has to see these things before one can visualize what Asiatic poverty really means.

There are elements of great strength in Urban India. There is an excellent system of courts, firmly established in the long period of British rule. Legal procedures are taken for granted. Legal institutions are recognized and respected. India is perhaps more firmly grounded in law and order than any of the other so-called underdeveloped countries.

Urban India has, moreover, a highly developed banking system with a strong central bank and knowledgeable people at its head. Urban India has a high-grade civil service, though many believe that some deterioration has set in following independence.

There is widespread nepotism both in government and in business, as can be expected in a country in which good positions are scarce. Traditionally a liberal education is prized above a technical education, though the latter is now on the increase. The head of the University Grants Commission has suggested that there are perhaps 750,000 unemployed college graduates in India.

Urban India has, in addition to its universities, colleges, and technical schools, a fair number of exceptionally high-grade private secondary schools and a rapidly growing number of state secondary schools, though of a lower quality. Elementary education is spreading in the urban population, though recent migrants from the rural area are still illiterate, as are many of the older members of the urban community.

Urban India has the social stratification common to all large cities to an intensified degree. There are the very rich and the miserably poor. There is a small and growing middle class—people who earn a family income of $800 or $900 per year. This of course is several times the *average* family income. There is also a growing class of skilled and semiskilled workers attached to the larger plants and firms. They have typically better income, better housing, and better working conditions than the mass of unskilled labor and those attached to the numerous small industries. Probably the gulf between the masses of unskilled labor on the one side and the skilled and middle-class income groups on the other side is becoming wider and wider.

Rural India

I said that there are two Indias—Urban India and Rural India. It is Rural India that makes the country as a whole unmistakably an underdeveloped country. Rural India, including the smaller towns, has an aggregate income of about $12 billion to be divided among a population of some 350 million. The per capita rural income is about $35 per year. The aggregate rural income is about equal to the aggregate urban income, but the rural population is almost six times greater. Urban income, per capita, is therefore about six times higher than rural income. But since in Urban India inequality of income distribution is possibly as great as, or greater than, in any other country in the world, the per capita income of the urban masses is not much above that of Rural India.

One can read books and articles on the Indian rural village, but one rarely gets a glimpse of what it is really like. Description fails, and even photographs help but little. One has to see the Indian village before one can begin to understand what rural poverty can be like. Everywhere the rural population lives in small villages consisting of about 600 people each. There are 600,000 of these rural farm villages. A village consists typically of a cluster of mud huts, though often a few of the houses are made from more substantial material. The mud hut contains usually from one to three small rooms. There are no windows, no tables, no chairs, no beds, no stoves, no furniture of any kind; only a few blankets and some pots and kettles. The family heirloom consists of jewelry and perhaps some brass or copper kettles. The floor is of hard-baked mud, almost like marble, at least in the dry season. The villagers sleep on the floor, they cook on the floor, they sit on the floor. The hearth consists of a few stones in a corner. There are no chimneys, and the smoke escapes through the door and through crevices in a leaky palm-leaf roof.

As one approaches a village, a large group of wholly or partly naked children crowd around. Typically they appear to be carefree. No school, nothing to do except to play in the dirt. Occasionally, especially in villages nearer the large cities, one finds a one-room schoolhouse, often open on two sides. The different age groups are rotated with one hour of instruction for each group. The male teacher receives $14 a month in salary. At seed time and harvest time the village adults are busy in the fields, but in the off season one frequently finds them napping under a tree or sitting in circles playing a game of dice. There is an immense amount of rural unemployment.

The population of India is growing at the rate of perhaps 8 or 9 million a year. In thirty years it may well reach, according to available estimates, 800 million, an increase of nearly 400 million. This *increase* amounts to twice the aggregate current population of the United Kingdom, West Germany, France, and Italy. And this population increase is occurring in a country that has a soil depleted and exhausted by centuries of bad farming. The soil has been robbed of its fertility. Half of the cow dung is used for fuel, and so lost to soil maintenance. The villagers share their meager food supply with 200 million sacred cows, 20 million of which are aged and diseased, and another 50 million are useless. Bullocks are widely used as draft animals. The cows produce some milk, but the yield is pitifully small. The animals are ill-nourished, as are the humans themselves. There is not enough food to go around. The sea around is full of fish, but the conscientious Hindu is a strict vegetarian. He may drink milk, but he may not eat meat, fish, fowl, or eggs.[1] Half-starved, he succumbs easily to disease. The average length of life is thirty-two years. Illiterate and superstitious, he tills a worn-out soil by primitive methods and obtains for his labor the lowest yield per acre of any country in the world.

And so India is a country of incredible contrasts—rich and poor, urban and rural. Urban and industrial India has its wealth, its culture, its universities, its banks, its commerce, its steel mills, its textile industry, its growng industrialism, and along with this its urban poverty. And then there is Rural India with its 60 million untouchables and its 600,000 mud

[1] The Indian population, however, includes 45 million Moslems and nearly 10 million Christians who eat meat, fish, fowl, and eggs.

villages—steeped in ignorance, superstition, squalor, and disease.

Much of the literature I have read about India seems to me to miss the mark. I have read a good deal about the "capital-output" ratio, about the "take-off" stage, about steel mills and heavy industry, about India competing with China in a race toward industrialization. This, it seems to me, starts at the wrong end. Industrialization? Yes, of course. Indeed, Urban India is already well on the way, and this development unquestionably deserves encouragement and support. But no good will come out of all this industrialization unless a massive rural program is undertaken in dead earnest. Whether India will survive or be lost to the free world will depend primarily upon what happens in the 600,000 mud villages.

An ambitious community-development program has been undertaken by the government. Rural India, under this plan, is divided into blocks of around 65,000 people each. Intensive work has been applied to a few pilot projects. But for the most part little has been accomplished in the 130,000 villages that on paper at least have been touched by the program. It is becoming increasingly clear that, lacking the necessary foundation of education, this program cannot be made self-sustaining. According to the Community Development Minister, of all the projects so far started, virtually nothing has been achieved in 50 per cent of the villages affected and very little in 40 per cent. In the remaining 10 per cent some improvement in agricultural methods has produced, it is reported, about 10 per cent higher yield per acre. The projects seek primarily to raise the level of agricultural practices, to build and operate schools, to build connecting roads, to introduce sanitation and public health measures. About 30,000 village-level workers, all high school graduates, have been given eighteen months of special training to prepare them for this work.

Often village opinion is hostile to these new developments,

and unless there is continual prodding, a relapse back to traditional practices is likely. This is certainly not surprising. An illiterate community with traditional cultural and religious convictions, firmly implanted from generation to generation, cannot easily be shunted over to a modern view of social values. Innovations that run counter to established dogmas and beliefs are feared lest they might anger various deities— the Hindu religion has hundreds of thousands of gods. Innovations might bring upon the helpless villagers scourges, pestilence, floods, or droughts. The power of tradition hangs on very firmly, and no change in social or economic practices can have much success until the chains that tie the villagers to their past are broken by an all-round system of universal education, including adult education.

Agricultural practices are controlled by custom and tradition. A villager is fearful of science. For many villagers insecticide is taboo, because all life is sacred. A new and improved seed is suspect. To try it is a gamble. Fertilizers, for example, are indeed a risk unless scientifically applied and with just the right amount of moisture. To adopt these untried methods might be to risk failure. And failure could mean starvation.

A villager may encounter social ostracism if he raises chickens and eggs for the tourist market. His friends and neighbors may exclude him from participation in community group activities. So what can one do except conform? Traditional practices are enforced under strong social pressures. Scientific health information is laughed at as obviously foolish and silly, since it is clearly in flat contradiction to long-established and firmly entrenched beliefs.

Moneylenders still make 90 per cent or more of the village loans at exorbitant interest rates despite state efforts to provide rural credit on more reasonable terms. The reason is that long-maintained personal relations between moneylenders and villagers cannot easily be broken off. The villager may be fearful that so important a man as the moneylender may in various ways do him harm. He may already be in debt to the moneylender. The moneylender charges more, but he can be depended upon and he may stand in good stead in the future. Newfangled credit connections may or may not work out, especially since it is a government scheme. The Indian villager, like his father and grandfather before him, is often highly suspicious of government officials.

The Role of Education

Progress, economic development, requires something much more fundamental than steel mills, important though these may be. It requires emancipation from tradition. Without such emancipation no significant improvement, social or economic, is possible. Rapid economic development, the take-off stage, the capital-output ratio, etc., can have little meaning as long as tradition retains its hold on the great rural masses. An adequate, universal, and compulsory system of education, including adult education, is a necessary prerequisite to progress. "The failure to search out and remove these cultural obstacles to economic development, and to adapt plans to what is culturally feasible, may very well retard economic development in the long run more than the lack of capital and competent technicians." [2] Education must be employed to "hasten the erosion of the traditional patterns of conduct obstructing the application of knowledge to practical problems." Yet it is common knowledge that "education is not faring well in many of the countries of Asia." The most important single question to ask is this: Will there be introduced soon, before it is too late, a sufficiently broad and thorough-going program of education "to ensure the development of

[2] Warren S. Thompson, *Population and Progress in the Far East,* University of Chicago Press, 1959, pp. 37, 40.

a more productive economy at anywhere near the speed these countries seem to expect"? [3]

Japan is a striking example of the role that education can play in economic development. The real basis of scientific agriculture in Japan (whose yields are among the highest in the world) is a system of universal and compulsory education. Introduced as early as 1868 (the date of the great revolution that ushered in the modern era in that country), a system of general education enabled Japan to break the hold of traditionalism and thereby to utilize the vast productive powers released by modern science. Japan did not begin with steel mills. She laid a solid foundation for economic development in her nationwide system of public education.

It is sometimes said that the people cannot be expected to wait for the slow processes of education. Progress must come quickly and spectacularly. People must be able to see quick results—big steel mills, power plants, etc. India must keep up with China. She must imitate the spectacular industrial progress of Russia. Yet I question whether the Indian villager can for long be much stirred by recitals of things done hundreds of miles away or by statistical charts showing the progress of Indian heavy industry. On the contrary, I am convinced that what the villagers want above all else is schools and teachers. True they also want a good well, a connecting road, a radio, and electricity. They want more food, and they want land reform. The tiller of the soil should own his own land.[4] Irrigation, fertilizer plants, electric power, transportation, and all that, must go forward hand in hand with education and agriculture. It must be a balanced program. Lest I be misunderstood, let me say emphatically that I

[3] *Ibid.*

[4] The land reform instituted by MacArthur under which landlordism was virtually wiped out was perhaps the greatest achievement of the American occupation of Japan. India needs very badly a similar sweeping land reform.

recognize the need for industrialization. But I do not believe that the Indian Second Five-Year Plan was a balanced program. There was far too little emphasis on education, agriculture, and population control. These should be made the primary goals. The other things should be developed as far and as fast as necessary to promote effectively the primary goals. Public investment in transportation, public utilities, power and irrigation, fertilizer and chemical plants is necessary even for the development of agriculture. Industrial progress goes hand in hand with agricultural progress.

It is sometimes said that primary emphasis on industrialization is essential in order to cure the problems of unemployment. I believe this to be a fallacy. And the reason is this. For every job created by industry several villagers press into the already overcrowded urban centers, thereby adding to the aggregate unemployment. This was actually taking place on a considerable scale under the Second Five-Year Plan. Unemployment is rapidly growing. And the movement of migrants into the cities provides no significant relief for the rural-population pressure. The rural population is growing at the rate of perhaps 6 to 7 million a year—nobody really knows. Any possible increase of migration to the cities could only slow down this rate of increase a little. And the greater the migration the more the urban unemployment will grow. "Any program which did not attempt to provide additional rural jobs for the expanding rural population would aggravate the already formidable problems of rural-urban differentials and migration, housing community facilities and social readjustment in the towns and cities." [5]

There is no lack of work to be done in the improvement of the rural villages and in the development and rejuvenation

[5] A. J. Coale and E. M. Hoover, *Population Growth and Economic Development in Low-income Countries*, Princeton University Press, 1958, pp. 76–77.

of the soil. What is lacking is rather the *will* and the *capacity* to tackle the job. And this will and this capacity can only be developed through a process of education. Village and agricultural improvement—better roads, better wells, better houses, some furniture, better seeds, better methods of tilling the soil, more and better use of fertilizer, more irrigation, and greater skill in getting the optimum use out of irrigation—all this is a herculean task. It is sheer nonsense to argue that the rural population must be moved to the cities in order to find useful work. There is plenty to be done in their own back yards.

The Role of Foreign Aid

Now this brings us to the matter of foreign aid. This is urgently needed. Yet I believe that the primary job—education and agriculture—can for the most part be done best by India herself. The construction work involved in the improvement of agriculture and in building schools for each of the 600,000 villages can be done by domestic labor and for the most part with domestic materials. This is true not only with respect to the construction work involved in community development projects, but even of much of the industrial construction which will be necessary in order to develop a scientific agriculture and all-round rural improvement. Irrigation, fertilizer plants, railroads, electricity, factory buildings—much of the construction which these projects involve can be performed by unskilled labor and with domestic materials. Considerable imports of equipment will of course be necessary.

How then does the United States fit into the picture? The most general statement of the case is, I think, as follows: Our aid to India should enable her to devote her productive resources as far as possible to her internal development without having to press any large part of her resources into a forced volume of exports designed to pay for the added imports which a program of development will require. It should be the function of our aid program to India to help her obtain these essential imports without drawing her resources away from her internal-development programs.

It will take some time before yields can be substantially increased even if a vigorous agricultural program is at once undertaken. In the meantime the program of development all around could be greatly accelerated by ensuring adequate nutrition for the entire population. A proposal is under consideration to build a large "food bank" with American aid.[6] The proposal involves the building up of a vast buffer stock of food grains designed to ensure adequate supplies over the period of the Third Five-Year Plan. These stocks could be made available in times of emergency and to fill the gap between (1) the food requirements of a population sufficiently well-nourished to carry forward a program of development and (2) the food supplies that India (in her present backward state of agricultural production) will be able to provide in the immediate future.

India already has received during recent years some 10 million tons of food grains from the United States under Public Law 480, which permits the sale of surplus farm products payable in Indian currency—the so-called "soft" loan. This program has necessitated the building of warehouses adequate to provide storage capacity. These warehouses have been built partly with American aid. The proposed program will require a substantial increase in such storage space.

Along with our grants we should play a role in helping India and other underdeveloped countries to make the best possible use of the foreign aid. We should of course not dictate. But

[6] *The New York Times*, December 21, 1959.

we could, as indeed we did in the case of the Marshall aid program, sit down with these countries and counsel with them in the formulation of their plans. And it is my judgment that we ought to throw the weight of our persuasion in the direction of a program which places primary emphasis on education and agriculture. And I do not believe that it will be possible even for our politicians to close their eyes for long to the urgent necessity of population control.

The public-health program in most of the underdeveloped countries has already considerably reduced the death rate, and this development will continue. The effect is an explosive growth of population. Programs of public health all over the world will have to come to grips—and that at once, not twenty years hence—with the high prevailing birth rates in all these countries. India has an official program of population control on paper, but the fact is that very little is being done. The government appears to be hoping for startling new scientific discoveries. This is a gamble, and anyway, without a massive attack on traditionalism (via education), it is doubtful if any birth-control technique, however perfected, could turn the tide. A rural villager, bound by tradition, feels uncertain about his future, unless he has as many as, say, three sons. In view of the high mortality of children this would mean on the average about six births per family. It is said that the Hindu religion presents no obstacle to birth control. In a technical sense this may be true, but tradition, based in part on religion, demands the preservation of the family, and so, in an uncertain world, several sons. Here as elsewhere many writers on India have missed the mark. They have failed to see, quite apart from religious dictates, the power of tradition.

The prospects for holding India within the free-world orbit are not bright. This is at any rate true, I believe, unless the scale of our economic aid is greatly increased. The slower processes of democratic measures cannot hope to compete with the forced speed-up of totalitarian communism if the emphasis is placed on heavy industry. In this area the communist methods bring quicker results. In the area of education and agriculture, however, the democratic methods may well prove more effective, as witness the progress of Japan. Broadly speaking, India's choice lies between Gandhiism and Marxism.

I have criticized the Indian Second Five-Year Plan on the ground that it placed a distorted emphasis on heavy industry. Yet the *absolute* amount allocated to heavy industry was probably not too large. What India needs is a much larger *aggregate* program, with the bulk of the increase going into education, agriculture, and population control. Yet any such enlarged program is quite impossible without a very considerable increase in foreign aid.

There are signs that the rich nations are growing richer and the poorer nations, if not poorer absolutely, at any rate poorer relatively. The gap is progressively growing. This issue cannot be pushed aside. The underdeveloped countries of the world demand to be heard. Humanitarianism developed in the late nineteenth century, but not because people were becoming kinder by nature. No, the fact is that the upper classes were forced into action by pressures applied from beneath. The working classes had reached a point in their development at which they demanded to be heard. Out of that ground swell of demand has grown the welfare state. And now the underprivileged countries of the world have reached a point in their development at which they also demand attention. The demand is pressed in upon us every day—at the United Nations and in all its associated organizations, at the foreign embassies situated in the underdeveloped capitals of the world, through diplomatic channels, and through the reports of journalists all over the world. We cannot open our morning newspapers without noting the call of the underprivileged countries. The welfare state has yet to be extended to the whole world. Foreign aid is imperative, but it represents nonetheless only a primitive approach to the far broader conception of world government and world interdependence.

The world has become too small to permit the continuance of so wide a diversity of wealth and income as that which now prevails. Rebellions, revolutions, riots—seething in Africa, in Asia, in the Near East, in Latin America—demand our attention. Their problems, at long last, have become our problems. A rich country in a world of poverty. There is no way of escape. This is the overwhelming problem which will inexorably haunt us more and more as we move on into the second half of the twentieth century.

CHAPTER 12

MONETARY POLICY
AND CAPITAL DEVELOPMENT

Monetary policy is one thing in a developed country. It is quite another matter in an underdeveloped country. And the same is true of fiscal policy. Similar courses of action are not always appropriate.

Capital Abundance versus Capital Scarcity

Highly developed countries like the United States are already equipped with a massive stock of capital goods. Plant and equipment in virtually every field of production are adequate to take care even of peak loads, and often, considerably in excess. The agelong preoccupation of economists with scarcity of resources is not the main problem. The problem is rather that of developing a market, as witness the ever-increasing drive of advertising.

But the problem of underdeveloped countries is something quite different. For them capital is scarce. They have not yet been able to assemble a vast stock of plant and equipment. Underdeveloped countries offer a fertile field of activity for the economist (steeped in classical tradition) who revels in scarcities. Everywhere there are grievous shortages—manufacturing producers' equipment, railroads and railway equip-

167

ment, highways, electric power, irrigation, farm equipment, dwellings, food.

Capital abundance in developed countries; capital scarcities in underdeveloped countries. Surely this suggests different policy approaches. Common sense tells us that this must be the case.

In a country like the United States there is no over-all shortage of funds available for investment. The American economy generates a vast flow of individual and corporate saving. Corporations are often able to finance two-thirds of their outlays on plant and equipment from depreciation allowances and one-third from retained earnings.

Corporate financial self-sufficiency is attainable only in highly developed countries. When a country is still in the early stages of industrial growth, the funds set aside as depreciation reserves are necessarily small because the accumulated capital stock to be depreciated is still insignificant. Capital formation is just beginning. But once a country has accumulated a vast stock of fixed capital—large plants and massive machinery—large depreciation allowances will at once begin to emerge.

Moreover, in rich and highly developed countries vast loan funds are available outside of the commercial banking system. Business firms can sell securities to the nonbanking public without recourse to bank loans. Funds can be borrowed directly from insurance companies, savings banks, and other financial intermediaries. Securities can be placed in the capital market. In a country like the United States the capital market is fed not merely from individual savings but also from the prodigious growth of pension funds and mutual investment companies. Vast sums can be raised in a rich and highly liquid society without applying for bank loans.

But this is not all. In a rich and highly liquid society the commercial banks can raise funds to lend to business even though the central banking system is exercising monetary restraint. They can sell their holdings of government securities to the nonbanking public—to insurance companies, savings banks, building and loan associations, pension funds, etc. Commercial banks in the United States have more than once, in recent years, unloaded billions of dollars of government securities and used the funds so obtained for loans to business.

The problem is not to get funds. The problem is to find adequate investment outlets. Industry after industry has excess capacity. Business is persistently under pressure to expand its market. Selling becomes a matter of primary concern in any highly developed country. It is not a question of scarcities. It is a question of superabundance and what to do with it.

A country that suffers from capital shortage should have a high rate of interest—a rate of interest that tends to attract capital from abroad and stimulates saving at home. Such a country has no need for a low rate of interest to stimulate investment. There is no shortage of investment opportunities and hence no need to foster a low rate of interest designed to open investment opportunities. Of these there are plenty. The problem is rather to find the funds necessary to finance investment.

In a highly developed country like the United States the matter is quite different. Here a low rate of interest is needed to open up investment outlets. In particular the frontiers of expansion—new technological developments—can best be exploited under conditions of high liquidity and low rates of interest.

Interest-rate Policy

The United States should normally expect to enjoy a low rate of interest. To be sure, to the extent that financial investors discount an inflationary trend, the nominal rate of interest will be higher than the real rate. But a country like the United States should not have to expect any substantial inflationary trend. If the exceptional bulges in investment, such as that of 1955–1957 can be overcome, we should be able to achieve a sufficiently stable level of prices (together with a healthy degree of uncertainty) to prevent any widespread gap between the nominal and the real rate of interest. The vast volume of savings that daily floods the capital markets—mutual funds, pension funds, savings deposits, insurance premiums, corporate depreciation funds, retained earnings— is a sufficient ground for the view that the real rate of interest ought to be low in a country like the United States.

Deliberate policy can, however, influence the rate. The Federal Reserve can add to the flow of investable funds by using the device of open-market purchases when a general increase in the money supply is needed to keep pace with a growing economy. It can augment investable funds further by absorbing a considerably larger amount of the public debt, offsetting any undue monetary expansionist effect by raising the reserve requirements. The Treasury could help to keep the nominal rate down by offering a purchasing-power savings bond. The purchasing-power guarantee would mean a somewhat lower nominal interest rate and possibly even a lower real rate.

Deliberate policy could, however, operate to raise the rate of interest. Excessive reliance on monetary policy to restrain inflationary tendencies has this effect. But to the extent that other restraining measures (fiscal policy and selective controls) are employed to check inflation, monetary policy can safely provide a greater degree of liquidity. It is, I believe, a fair statement that the Eisenhower Administration has relied excessively on monetary restraint. Both monetary policy and debt management have been employed in a manner that has raised the rate of interest to an unduly high level.

The Treasury has tried to concentrate on long-term bond issues in boom periods when the rate of interest tends to be high. This policy raises the interest charges in the marketable public debt, and this could reach a point at which income distribution is unfavorably affected.

Long-term bonds, to the extent that it is deemed desirable to lengthen the maturity of the public debt, should be issued in relatively slack periods when interest rates are low. The Federal Reserve should counter the stiffening effect which such a policy would have on interest rates by providing ample liquidity. The fact that debt-management policy in this case would work counter to monetary policy is no valid objection. The Federal Reserve is amply able to provide all the liquidity that may be desired, regardless of Treasury policy. There is no good reason to suppose that debt-management policy and monetary policy must necessarily supplement each other.[1]

These reforms in debt-management policy would provide three beneficial results: (1) the interest cost of the marketable public debt would be reduced, (2) interest-rate fluctuations would be less severe, and (3) over the long run the level of long-term interest rates would be lower.

Budget Surpluses and Interest Rates

A new argument was injected in the interest-rate debate in connection with the Budget message presented to Congress in January, 1960. The President proposed for fiscal 1961 a budgetary surplus of $4.2 billion. Such a budget surplus is usually

[1] Economists have usually argued that the Treasury should issue long-terms in boom periods and short-terms in depression. The effect of such a policy is to accentuate fluctuations in the rate of interest. To this I am opposed. But for those who rely primarily upon monetary policy, the procedure indicated is indeed the logical one.

justified on the basis of the requirements of a balance of aggregate demand in relation to the aggregate supply of goods and services. In this case, however, a new note was struck. It was argued that the budget surplus was needed to increase the flow of investable funds, and so to promote a lower rate of interest.

The budget surplus is thus intended not to restrain aggregate demand, but rather to switch funds from consumption to investment. This could well happen, to a degree at least, if the budget surplus was used to retire government debt held by the nonbanking public. Even here it is possible, however, that part of the funds paid out to the public would be hoarded. And if the budget surplus were used to retire the public debt held by the Federal Reserve System, the effect would clearly be to curtail aggregate demand unless the Federal Reserve countered by open-market purchases.

If the surplus was used to retire debt held by commercial banks, the first effect would be to reduce both the assets and the deposit liabilities of the banks and so cause a contraction of the money supply. But since member-bank reserve balances would not be reduced, the banks would (after the debt retirement) be able to extend loans to business in an equal amount. In this case the net effect of the Treasury surplus could tend to cause a switch from consumption to investment.

The suggestion that a budget surplus should deliberately be planned for the purpose of reducing the rate of interest emphasizes the point that fiscal policy is not limited merely to the achievement of monetary equilibrium. Monetary equilibrium means an over-all balance between aggregate demand and the aggregate supply of all goods and services. A budget surplus, designed to lower the rate of interest and to stimulate investment, is not intended to contain inflationary pressures. It shifts expenditures from consumption to investment. But it is neutral with respect to inflation. Restrictive monetary policy is on the contrary designed to raise the rate of interest in order to restrain investment. Countercyclical accelerated depreciation policy would also aim to restrict investment. Moreover, a tax on investment, to be applied only in periods of an excessive investment spurt, has the same end in view. But a budget surplus implemented so as to lower the rate of interest is designed to shift the use of resources, not to control aggregate demand.

Under certain circumstances it may well be wise policy to use a budgetary surplus to retire debt held by the non-banking public. Such a policy, backed up by an easy-money policy, would tend to stimulate investment. The two policies combined would add to the liquidity of the community and would tend to promote a lower rate of interest. The budget surplus would act as a restraint on consumption assuming the appropriate kinds of taxes. Investment would expand; consumption would contract; aggregate demand might remain the same.

Forced Saving for Underdeveloped Countries

Fiscal policy takes on a different hue in underdeveloped countries. In such countries it is not possible to induce the amount of saving urgently needed to finance essential investment merely by offering a high rate of interest, important though this may well be. Voluntary saving is just not adequate. For this reason, underdeveloped countries have found by experience that development projects cannot find adequate financing except through a judicious use of central-bank credit.

In the case of underdeveloped countries the really important question is not whether or not central-bank credit should be used for development, but rather what is the optimum degree of inflationary pressure which may legitimately be exerted in order to pump the necessary amount of forced saving out of the community. Forced saving results whenever an expansion of credit is placed in the hands of development corporations. This puts a squeeze upon consumers. The whole community is at one stroke put to work earning income and at the same time subjected to a tax—the tax imposed by rising prices.

For underdeveloped countries the alternative is often stagnation and unemployment. Development puts people to work, creates income, a part of which is taken away for investment via the rise in prices. I repeat, for underdeveloped countries the question is not inflation versus rigid price stability. The question is what *degree* of inflation is optimum for development. Voluntary saving is inadequate. It needs to be supplemented to some extent by forced saving.

Capitalism in its early stages, notably in England, grew and developed in no inconsiderable degree from forced saving. Witness the enclosure movements and the early-nineteenth-century profits based on the exploitation of labor, including woman and child labor, prior to the development of factory legislation and trade-unionism. Similarly, though by different methods, Russia has been squeezing capital formation out of the productive process through the policy of suppressing consumption. In the underdeveloped countries capital formation is squeezed out of a limited aggregate income through the process of inflation. Forced saving is common to all these historical processes of capital formation.

Forced saving is unnecessary for a country like the United States. But for underdeveloped countries the matter is quite otherwise. But how far can forced saving be pushed without upsetting the productive process? That is a difficult question. Experience does give, within limits, at least a partial answer.

The well-nigh astronomical inflations of Chile and Bolivia clearly have had a disruptive effect on output and growth.

On the other hand, Brazil's inflation, of about 30 per cent per year, has not prevented a substantial growth rate of around 5½ per cent per year. Argentina, with about the same inflation record, has a poor growth and output record. Turkey, with a 7 per cent increase in prices per year, shows a 6½ per cent increase in output.

The Case of Mexico and Japan

Mexico, everything considered, presents perhaps the best case of a successful policy of forced saving. With an inflation record of 15 per cent per year from 1940 to 1950 and of 8 per cent per year from 1950 to 1957, her growth in output has averaged around 6½ per cent per year.

No one can visit Mexico without being impressed with her progress—greater diversification, development of new industries, irrigation, highways, railroads, electric generating capacity, imports of capital goods, inflow of foreign funds, net tourist earnings. The record is there to see. Would Mexico have done as well with less forced saving? Possibly. But this type of argument can be applied to any country and to any policy.

Had Mexico produced the invested savings via a tax on incomes generally (and with no inflation), critics would probably have applauded. But it is far from being clear that such a tax would have been a superior method of extracting investment funds from the country. The inflationary forced-saving method has the great advantage that it creates jobs even while by the same stroke the inflationary tax is imposed. An effort to raise the funds via a direct tax on incomes might well have produced stagnation. The Mexican experience lends support to the view that for underdeveloped countries, with utterly inadequate flows of voluntary saving, the inflationary forced-saving method may, up to some indefinite limits, prove advantageous. For such countries there may well be such a thing as an optimum degree of inflationary forced saving. Such an optimum rate, if there indeed be one, would doubtless vary greatly from country to country.[2]

Now just as I do not favor any price stabilization mandate for the United States, so also I do not favor any announced official policy by any underdeveloped country to pursue any given program of inflationary forced saving. Rigid formulas will not do. In these matters all countries must learn to play, so to speak, by ear. It is like driving a car on a tricky highway. You have to feel your way. The road changes and you have to adjust accordingly. You can't turn the steering wheel over to a formula. You have to apply judgment. Discretionary decisions have to be made. Mistakes have to be rectified. The search for the "optimum rate" is likely to be difficult and elusive.

Japan is another country with a long record of successful inflationary forced saving. From 1886 to 1940 Japan experienced a sixfold increase in prices—an annually compounded rate of nearly 3½ per cent. From 1886 to 1913 the rate was 3¼ per cent per year; from 1913 to 1940 it was 3½ per cent. Industrial production increased at a rate of about 15 per cent per year from 1890 to 1910 and about 12 per cent per year from 1910 to 1940.[3]

Neither Japan nor Mexico undertook a *deliberate* program of inflation. Instead they undertook a program of economic development. In the process something happened to prices.

[2] See in this connection the objective and highly informative article in the May, 1953, *Monthly Review* of the New York Federal Reserve Bank. In contrast, the article in the August, 1959, issue attempts to draw conclusions that must be regarded as at least doubtful. Precisely the opposite conclusions could equally well be drawn from the data presented: The truth appears to lie somewhere in between.

[3] K. Ohkawa, *The Growth Rate of the Japanese Economy*, Kinokuniya Bookstore Co., 1957.

The result might not be the best, but it conceivably approached the maximum that was attainable. It is even possible, Paul Samuelson has suggested, that we could discover politico-economic models for underdeveloped countries according to which (1) if the rate of inflation falls below a certain point, the government is in danger of falling and (2) if the rate rises above some critical point, the government likewise tends to fall—a kind of "disequilibrium-equilibrium model of such nations' inflationary development." [4]

[4] Paul Samuelson, in *Problems of United States Economic Development*, Committee for Economic Development, New York, 1958.

Appendixes

APPENDIX A

THE SWEEPING RISE
OF URBANIZATION

Let me begin by setting aside two problems which are likely to spring at once into the mind of the reader as the most important issues to be faced by the United States in the next twenty years.[1]

Inflation, I think, is not the most important of these. We may well experience an upward drift of prices in these two decades, but it is not likely to become a serious problem. There are many powerful stabilizing forces inherent in the American economy. Not the least of these is its astonishing capacity to pour out an abundant supply of goods of all kinds. The American economy is singularly fortunate in that it contains no serious structural bottlenecks—the bane of all inflation-sensitive economies. And the American economy exhibits a capacity, both corporate and individual, to generate vast streams of saving at full-employment levels. These are powerful safeguards against inflation. Moreover, the public is conscious, as never before, of this problem. We shall have price adjustments to a rapidly expanding output, but we shall not,

[1] Alvin H. Hansen, in *Problems of United States Economic Development*, Committee for Economic Development, New York, 1958, pp. 325–330.

I think, have inflation. We shall not achieve perfection, but we shall manage this problem reasonably well.

Nor is the highly important problem of adequate aggregate demand likely to be the most important problem. By this I emphatically do not mean that this vital matter can be allowed to take care of itself. The private economy, on its own, cannot be depended upon to generate adequate steam to provide full employment. The matter will not automatically solve itself. Nevertheless, despite the continued survival of quite obsolete ideas about fiscal policy, there appears to be no likelihood that any administration, whether Republican or Democratic, will again tolerate mass unemployment and serious depression. Thinking on these matters has profoundly changed. Policies that formerly were regarded as axiomatic are now as archaic as the horse and buggy. Policies that formerly instilled fear and consternation are now regarded as part of a stabilizing mechanism. The rules of the game have profoundly changed. Instead of a babel of voices, we now witness well-nigh a consensus. The tools are at our command, and we have the will to use them. We shall not reach perfection, but we shall manage this problem also, I venture to believe, reasonably well.

What then is the most important economic problem which will confront the United States in the next twenty years? It is, I believe, the problem created by the sweeping increase in urbanization.

Census statistics indicate that about 60 per cent of the population of the United States now live in 168 standard metropolitan areas. These areas (which include the large urban centers and their suburbs) account for nearly all the 19 million increase in population which has occurred in the United States as a whole from 1950 to 1957. It may thus be anticipated that these 168 metropolitan areas will grow from the current 100 million to perhaps 160 million in twenty years.

This tidal wave will throw up economic, fiscal, and social

problems, the magnitude of which we have scarcely yet glimpsed. Unfortunately the United States is peculiarly unfitted by temperament and historical background, and by our obsolete, "Balkanized" network of multiple local governments, to face this problem.

The great industrial centers of the United States have been allowed to spawn and grow like Topsy. We have no tradition of city planning, no deep sense of aesthetic values, of spaciously laid-out squares with fountains, landscaping, flowers, shrubs or trees, no pride in architecturally satisfying public buildings. We have traditionally regarded expenditure on such things as economically wasteful. Even our pitifully inadequate post-office buildings have served as a butt for jokes about wasteful extravagance. The United States has not since colonial days been able to "afford" elegant and artistic public buildings. And even today when it produces half the world's output, it can still not afford these amenities.

A distinguished city-planning consultant and past president of the American Institute of Planners felt constrained to confess that aesthetic grounds for supporting urban-development programs are likely to be laughed off. Thus, in order to carry any weight, it becomes necessary to find utilitarian arguments —economic and medical. Breathing space—easy reach of green fields—could perhaps be made acceptable to American value standards, he reflects, if they could be justified on medical and health grounds.[2]

The upward surge of the urban-metropolitan population will of necessity involve—whether haphazardly carried out through compromised maneuvers between conflicting interest groups or by some reasonable approach to scientific city planning—a stupendous program of demolition and rebuilding. There will be elevated express highways and surface arteries

[2] John T. Howard, "Basic Research Problem of the Urban Metropolitan Region," The Regional Science Association.

and approaches. These things will indeed be done in some manner, though often it is to be feared in a ruthless fashion, and always with a lagged adjustment to the urgent needs and aspirations of the community.

The central economic problem springing from this development will be that of finance. The tidal wave of urban growth will push to the foreground as never before the problem of Federal-State-local fiscal relations.

The Federal government is already deep in urban redevelopment, and no amount of talk about shifting public functions to State and local bodies will dispose of its responsibilities. The impending growth of metropolitan areas will be so torrential in scope and magnitude that out of it drastic changes will have occurred at the end of two decades in Federal-State-local finances. We shall witness a hard political fight between restrictionist States'-righters and Federal expansionists. This fight will determine in large part how adequately the needs of the rapidly growing urban communities will be met.

The outcome of this struggle will moreover in large measure set the goals toward which our society is moving. Will the United States in the next twenty years move further and further into an unending merry-go-round of ever-bigger and more ostentatious mechanical gadgets, or will we choose to devote a much larger part of our manpower and resources to the nurture and growth of a culturally rich society? It may even be that the pursuit of this latter goal could check the explosive rise of concentrated urbanism and lead to a more sensible decentralization of population.

It is said that the United States has broken through the sound barrier of technological progress. We are confronted with the prospect of such an inundation of mechanical "toys" as to drown out the things of the mind and the spirit. This has already reached a kind of national insanity (*vide* 350-horse-power cars stretching halfway across a block).

The conflict, it must frankly be stated, is in no small degree one between a rigidly private-enterprise point of view and a social-welfare point of view. If more and more of our productive energies are devoted to building culturally rich communities, the fraction of the Gross National Product going through the public fisc will grow. A larger proportion of the population will be engaged in educational and recreational activities, medical research, health centers and hospitals, and in creative work in all the arts. The basis of education will be broadened not only for children but also for adults. Anyone who has had any contact with adult-education centers in the United States must have been impressed with the meager, crowded, and dismal facilities that are available and the low salaries and inferior quality of instruction. If a visitor from abroad saw nothing of the United States except these centers, he would have to conclude that the United States must be a very impoverished country with a depressingly low standard of living.

The building of a culturally rich community means that we will have to devote far more effort to make our urban areas places in which to live, not merely places where material goods are produced. This means inevitably the growth of the public sector. Factories making things will grow absolutely, but they will play, I venture to hope, a smaller role in our economic life relative to the GNP. If, on the other hand, this development path takes the road of more and more mechanical toys, the private sector will grow at the expense of community activities. The role of private enterprise is peculiarly that of manufacturing, transporting, and selling things. The role of the public sector is to provide the physical environment and community activities needful for good urban living. If private enterprise grows in the next twenty years at the expense of the public sector, our urban areas will become even more mechanically minded than they are today. And we are starting this twenty-year period from a point at which the backlog of community-oriented needs is already very great.

It is a striking fact that Governor Stevenson's program, dubbed "pie in the sky" by his opponents, was so cautious as to urge only a proportionate share (if indeed that much) in the increase of GNP for schools, hospitals, and public-welfare projects and programs in general.

The choice of goals to which I have referred will also help to solve another problem which already has become a major point of controversy—high or low rates of interest. Whether or not continued full employment tends to boost wages to an uneconomic level in relation to productivity, there is growing evidence, throughout the Western world, that it is producing by the aid of currently prevailing policies an uneconomic high level of interest rates. This is a very serious matter, and it affects profoundly the task of building urban communities.

One of the really great structural gains of the postwar period was the boost to economic expansion and growth which a low rate of interest and high all-round liquidity provided. A low rate of interest is favorable to a more equitable distribution of income. It makes feasible pushing to the hilt the investment outlets opened up by technological advances. As David Hume said long years ago, a low rate of interest is a "sign almost infallible of a flourishing condition of a people."

This interest-rate matter is of course a long and technical story, and I wish only to say here that the growth of our large urban centers will require large flotations of securities at all levels of government. A high rate of interest would tend to check and restrict the range and scope of the public activities needed to direct the trend of urban life toward the goals of a truly high-standard country.

Having reached the automation age of technical progress, the United States can afford to relegate material goods to a secondary role. It can afford to build urban communities that measure up to the great values which the knowledge and experience of the ages have pronounced good.

APPENDIX B

TRENDS AND CYCLES
IN ECONOMIC ACTIVITY

Professor Fellner[1] has written an important book—one that measures up, in the analytical parts, to the high standards we have learned to expect from him. I am in almost complete agreement with his fundamental analysis, and indeed very much of it is a forceful presentation of a point of view which I have long maintained. The author clearly presents the basic factors underlying economic growth. His analysis of the varying impact of different *kinds* of improvements in the marginal productivity of capital and labor is especially valuable.

Nevertheless, I am very much afraid that this review article will appear more critical than I would like it to be. As might no doubt be expected, I am not quite happy about his policy conclusions and recommendations, and this is not altogether due to the fact that my prejudices (temperamental bias or, if you prefer, personal value judgments) are somewhat different from his. But more of this later.

First, the analysis of the conditions underlying dynamic equilibrium—the growth process.

The western world has indeed witnessed a span of unprece-

[1] *Trends and Cycles in Economic Activity: An Introduction to Problems of Economic Growth,* by William Fellner. New York: Henry Holt and Company. 1956. Pp. xiv, 411. $5.00.

dented material progress in the period 1825–1955. It has not been one of uninterrupted growth. Cyclical disturbances constitute deviations from dynamic equilibrium. Of these Professor Fellner takes full account. It may be questioned, however, whether he is not somewhat overly sanguine with respect to his view (a view that at several points he himself seems to contradict) that "thus far there has been no tendency toward chronic unemployment of appreciable size in the industrialized economies."

Growth and progress there has been. And the primary factors underlying this growth, the author rightly points out, were: (1) improvements in the productive process—technological advances, population growth, net additions to natural resources—all of which served to offset the classical law of diminishing returns; (2) mobility of resources—adjustments of the internal structure of the economy including wage, price, and interest-rate adjustments; and (3) a flexible supply of money and credit. When properly functioning, these factors should induce a volume of investment sufficient to match new savings.

Despite the statement referred to above (no tendency to date toward chronic unemployment), Fellner does point out that the protracted depressions of the post-Napoleonic decades, the depressions of the 1870's and the 1890's, and the Great Depression, may have had something to do with the fact that the technological and organizational revolution in already established fields had spent itself, while in new fields the transformation process had not yet reached a stage where it could exert a sufficient upward pull on the economy. Elsewhere he refers to the decline in population growth, the decline in net additions to natural resources, and to a tendency at times for improvements to be too capital-saving—all of which factors would tend to diminish investment opportunities.

But long-lasting insufficiency of the improvement process is not, he thinks, the only cause of protracted depressions. Inadequate mobility of factors may play a part. In the building-cycle downswing, resources cannot be shifted quickly to other fields. An inadequate money supply may slow down the rate of expansion. And a mere *slowing down* may cause a contraction. Important industries depend on a *rate of growth*. All these factors are important, but the sluggishness, in certain periods, of the improvement process as an offset to diminishing returns is the main factor stressed by the author.

The long-run growth tendency has very largely, says Fellner, been a consequence of the fact that technological and organizational improvements have exceeded those anticipated by the Ricardian doctrine. These improvements have tended to keep planned investment at the needed level to match full-employment savings. He denies the classical doctrine—Say's Law—that in the long run, savings cannot become excessive in relation to investment. The adjustment has come primarily from the improvement factor, and not from the price-wage adjustment-mechanism or changes in the propensity to save.

Flexibility of interest rates and of the price-wage structure has played a role. But neither empirical data nor common observation makes it safe, he believes, to assume that the interest rate mechanism or price-wage adjustments *in themselves* would have turned the trick. The Ricardian school was unduly optimistic about the ability of the interest rate and price-wage mechanism to achieve the necessary result within a reasonable period of time. But it was unduly pessimistic concerning the improvement factor. Thus the Ricardian school was optimistic about the avoidance of chronic unemployment but pessimistic with respect to the prospect for continued growth.

In the very, very long run, says Professor Fellner, the classical equilibrating mechanism might conceivably work out even without the improvement factor. But if future history should test this hypothesis, the hardships of an extended period would probably lead to a political collapse of the private enterprise system.

Fellner accordingly does not accept Say's Law as valid whether for the short run or the long run. He believes that most contemporary economists are convinced, as he is, that the equilibrating process, based on the interest rate and price-wage mechanisms, would not alone perform satisfactorily. If investment activity became exhausted, the propensity to save might continue, and therefore effective demand would fall below the full-employment level. It follows therefore that continued growth requires an *improvement* mechanism which will effectively offset the tendency toward diminishing returns.

It could be argued that the classicals' faith in the interest-rate, wage-price adjustment was to a greater degree justified in their time than now. Yet it is questionable, says Professor Fellner, whether conditions under capitalism *ever* were such as to warrant the assumption that the hardships of the classical adjustment process would have been accepted. They would clearly not be accepted now. Chronic insufficiency of profitable investment opportunities, due to an inadequate improvement factor, would lead to radical institutional change.

To the neo-classicals of the late nineteenth century, cessation of growth due to insufficient offsets to diminishing returns seemed exceedingly remote. But if it should ultimately come, Say's Law—conceived as a long-run proposition—was believed to insure continued full employment. For long-run analysis there existed for the neo-classicals no problem of a discrepancy between full-employment savings and investment. Say's Law, says Fellner, was never intended as a short-run proposition.

I fully agree with Fellner here, and this is a point that

should be stressed. Even now one finds in the current journal articles the contention that Keynes, in attacking Say's Law, was beating a dead horse. This is quite wrong. From Mill to Marshall, Knut Wicksell, and many others, up to Keynes, it can easily be shown that Say's Law was firmly upheld as a long-run proposition (see my *Guide to Keynes*, pages 11–14). Prominent anti-Keynesians still uphold this view.

"In some 'secular long-run' Say's Law may well possess theoretical validity." The discrepancy between savings and investment might simply be eliminated by an adjustment of saving habits to a climate created by the absence of adequate investment opportunities. But the deficiency of investment would at first result in a reduction of employment and income, and this condition could persist long enough to cause irreparable damage. "This is the sense in which we shall accept the 'Keynesian' Proposition that the long-run insufficiency of planned investment is conceivable." While he does not believe it should be anticipated, still he concludes that it is "essential to realize that significant long-run insufficiency of private investment is a possibility." Even in the nineteenth century when admittedly the *extensive* improvement factors were far stronger than today, the prolonged insufficiency of private investment was at times so serious, he believes, that under political conditions (strong labor organizations, etc.) such as now obtain, the private enterprise system could not have survived.

Should a significant long-run insufficiency of private investment develop, then, in Fellner's view, the system of private enterprise is doomed. The reason is, as he sees it, that such a chronic insufficiency could not be offset by fiscal policy within the private enterprise framework. The "institutions of a profit economy lose their essential functions if the growth process is sustained mainly by government investment."

Not only must the improvement process be *adequate*. The

growth process also requires, says Fellner, the adjustment of the *character* of the improvements to the relative resource scarcities existing or developing in the economy. One cannot rely upon the price mechanism alone to make the necessary adjustment. In Western economies the capital stock has been rising at a much higher rate than the labor supply—roughly about twice as fast. And when the rate of population growth declined, the rate of growth of the capital stock declined in about the same proportion. Improvements may affect not merely the capital productivity schedules but also the labor productivity schedules. If an improvement raised the capital productivity schedule this would indeed increase investment and so tend to raise the demand for labor. But if such improvements *also* have the effect of drastically supplanting labor, the net effect could be to lower the labor productivity schedule and to cause chronic unemployment. "It is not enough that improvements should be sufficiently 'cost-saving.' An additional requirement is that their character—their impact on the marginal productivity schedules of the various factors of production—should by and large accord with the relative resource scarcities in the economy."

Apart from frictional unemployment, there are two kinds of unemployment in the modern world. By and large, one kind afflicts advanced countries like the United States, and the other underdeveloped countries like Italy or India. The first is due to inadequate demand resulting from an inadequate *flow* of investment—an inadequate volume of *current* capital formation to mop up full employment savings. The insufficiency of investment reaches back into the past—and is due in part to an excessive *stock* of capital.[2] In part it reaches into

---

[2] I am told that Sir Dennis Robertson recently got off the following witticism: What is needed is a large *increment* of population growth but no larger population! He might have added that periodically advanced countries have needed a large *flow* of investment, but no net additions to the *stock*.

the future, and is due to an inadequate improvement factor
—failure to lift the marginal productivity of capital schedule
sufficiently to stimulate a volume of investment adequate to
absorb full-employment saving. The failure of the improvement factor may be due to an inadequate *volume* of technological progress or to inadequate growth of the complementary
factors—population and natural resources. Or it may be due
to the wrong kind of improvements—wrong for this kind of
society. Thus improvements that are capital-saving only add
to the already surfeited capital supply.

The other kind of unemployment—that of underdeveloped
countries—presents altogether a different picture. Here the
situation is quite the reverse. Far from there being too large
a *stock* of capital, the trouble is that the stock is not large
enough. There is not enough equipment to employ the entire
labor force. Whereas, in the case of rich and developed
economies, investment has often been inadequate to offset
full employment saving, in poor underdeveloped countries
saving is inadequate to raise quickly the stock of capital to
anything approaching the amount needed. In the rich, developed countries, the propensity to save is at times too large
in relation to the volume of profitable investment and so
aggregate demand is inadequate. In the poor underdeveloped
country, the propensity to save is insufficient to provide adequate plant and machinery for full employment. In the rich
country the *stock* of capital may be too large, but the rate
of capital formation too low. In the poor country the *stock*
of capital is too small but the *rate* of investment tends to outrun the low volume of current saving. The rich country needs
improvements which raise the marginal productivity of capital
—improvements which tend to make capital scarce. The poor
country needs capital-saving improvements—improvements
which tend to make capital plentiful.

By and large this is what Professor Fellner is saying in his long and somewhat technical discussion of the role of (a) *volume* of capital formation and (b) *character* of capital formation upon employment, growth, and progress.

He does not accept the Harrod-Domar assumption of *constancy* of the ratio (a) of saving to income even over the long run, or (b) of the output increment per unit of new investment. Nevertheless, it is important to note, he does assume that in a growing economy, an appreciable or consistent tendency toward diminishing returns must be offset by *improvements* because the adjustability of the relative income shares and of the interest rate and wage-price mechanism is limited. It is the improvement factor that must primarily make the adjustment, not the price-cost system or savings habits.

So much for the improvement factor (both in terms of quantity and quality) as it applies to rich and poor countries. We need now to consider a little more fully the other two conditions underlying adequate growth at full employment —mobility of resources and a flexible money supply.

Observable trends indicate that, so far, there has been enough long-run flexibility and mobility in Western economies to assure gradual removal of prohibitive bottlenecks. There are lags to be sure, and new shifts continually call for further adjustment. The result, far from perfect dynamic equilibrium, represents a long-run tendency toward *lowered* paths of dynamic equilibrium.

Fellner believes that some recent institutional changes (trade unions, farm programs) tend to slow down and might conceivably even block the mobility of resources. However, he feels that it would take a good deal of pessimism to expect that these difficulties will grow to a point where disturbances would decisively interfere with the growth process.

The third condition underlying growth is an elastic money supply. Here legal and institutional factors must be compatible with proper regulation of the money supply. Deviations from this principle do not seem so far to have blocked the long-run growth process.

Monetary and fiscal policy, Fellner believes, is more likely to err somewhat in the inflationary direction. The long-run trend is likely to be tilted upward. However, if the slope is mild, this may not impair the efficiency of Western economies.

None of the three underlying growth conditions relates *explicitly* to adequate aggregate demand. Should we not add this as a fourth requirement for continued growth? Fellner thinks not. If the relative scarcities have been overcome— if the improvement factor is adequate, both quantitatively and qualitatively, if factors are reasonably mobile, and if the money supply is properly adjusted—then aggregate demand will necessarily prove to be adequate.

This conclusion follows, of course, from the premises. The vital question, however, relates to the first premise—the improvement factor—as Fellner elsewhere freely admits.

It may be noted at this point, however, that Fellner's position, as here stated, runs the risk of operating at the wrong end of the circle. Adequate mobility of factors, for example, does indeed promote adequate aggregate demand. But let us look at it the other way around. Adequate aggregate demand promotes mobility of resources. When demand is adequate, resources are easily shifted to the growing sectors. This the war experience taught us. When demand is adequate, cartel and other market restrictions tend to vanish, as do also trade union restrictions on output. When jobs are plentiful, the tendency "to make a job last" softens. The older doctrine, that the place to start is with mobility, has the thing turned upside down. The problem of relative prices and mobility of factors really becomes manageable only under conditions of adequate aggregate demand, not the other way around. It is fair to add, that while Fellner stresses (and rightly so) mobility of resources and flexible relative prices, he does not believe that by operating *primarily* on these (including the interest-rate and wage-price mechanism) adequate aggregate demand can be assured.

Professor Fellner definitely does not pin his faith on wage reductions. This is true not only of wage reductions which give rise to expectations of further reductions but also of those that are believed to have run their course. The Pigou effect is heavily discounted. It is, he believes, uncertain and undependable since the real worth of corporations and many individuals tends to shrink with falling prices. Also the increased liquidity (in real terms) may not help, since the money released from transactions may go into hoards and not into the loan fund. Also he doubts that the redistributional effect of lower real wage rates (if indeed wage rates should fall more than prices) will reduce unemployment, since the resulting prospect of reduced consumption will tend to weaken the incentive to invest. Finally, general wage reductions can scarcely fail to cause serious social friction.

So, we return to the most critical matter—that of the improvement factor. A chronic weakness of this factor would, Fellner believes, lead straight to the stagnation thesis. At the very least, the long-run automatic adjustment of savings habits (if it developed at all) would act so slowly that our social system could not survive the interval.

Fellner does not believe it feasible to arrive at categoric conclusions with respect to the future of the improvement factor. The population growth of the nineteenth century will certainly not repeat itself. The rate of increase of the stock of natural resources available for economic development has been losing in significance and will undoubtedly become smaller. Yet we are learning to render exploitable a stock of resources hitherto inaccessible. In this sense, it is not certain that the present century will turn out to have brought out less resource acquisition than did the nineteenth century.

Throughout the volume, Fellner repeatedly points to indicators of a possible accelerated rate of technological-organizational progress. Still, everything considered, long-lasting depressions such as we have had in the past can be caused by an insufficient improvement rate. And such insufficiency may last for many years. Moreover, during a period of several decades, the intervals of vigorous improvement may be fewer and weaker. Thus longish periods of hard times may occur—the average level of activity falling below capacity production.

Thus if planned private investment is too low in relation to the propensity to save, the basic requirement for maximum growth is violated. But could not this deficiency of investment be filled by the government?

Fellner says no. Compensatory fiscal policy, designed to reduce (a) the "severity of fluctuations," and (b) the "special hardships" of deep and long-lasting depressions, and (c) small imbalances of a chronic character, is indeed, he thinks, both feasible and desirable. But should a chronic condition develop, governmental effort to fill the gap would only bring ruin to the private enterprise system. Yet extended periods of "substantial unemployment have become intolerable. If periods of this sort should recur, the private enterprise system would be very unlikely to survive. The fateful consequences of the nineteen-thirties tell a very convincing story." In present circumstances a much less serious depression would cause radical changes in the social order.

In this connection, Fellner discusses deficit financing and compensatory fiscal policy. Perhaps inadvertently, he muddies the argument a good deal by an unfortunate terminology. He interchanges "deficit financing" and "compensatory fiscal policy" as though they were synonymous, which is far from being the case. And with respect to the former, "loan financing" is in fact better terminology, not only because it has fewer emotional overtones, but also because it is more accurate, since budgetary deficits can be one thing when capital budgets are employed and another thing when they are not. When a corporation borrows for development projects we do not call it "deficit financing."

The policy discussion begins with an examination of the limitations of "deficit financing." First it is suggested that "deficit financing" is wholly incapable of reducing unemployment in capital-poor (underdeveloped) countries. Most economists would go along with this up to a point, but Fellner puts the case a bit too strongly. A moderate amount of deficit-financed (even central-bank-financed) public outlay on development projects—power resources, railroads, roads, basic industries—may well be in order even though it is accompanied by some increase in prices. Such a policy may accelerate the growth of the capital stock. Before we become too dogmatic on this point, a careful study should be made of the history of underdeveloped countries since 1940. Mexico is a case in point. She has had a considerable inflation, though far below that of Chile; and her growth and expansion (compared with that in Chile) have been remarkable. It is, I should say, probable that there is some *optimum* degree of "deficit-financed" public development projects—indeed even some optimum degree of price rise—for undeveloped countries.

Fellner holds that "deficit financing" may usefully be employed in developed countries suffering from a temporary deficiency of investment. Yet even here "compensatory fiscal policy" (here as elsewhere he uses the terms interchangeably) has, he believes, certain limitations. A fiscal policy guarantee of full employment would, he fears, lead to constant pressure for higher wages.

History discloses an interesting display of danger signals raised against fiscal expansionist policies. Perhaps the leading current danger signal is that of wage pressures. Wise as this may well be, it can be, and perhaps has been, overdone. In the first place, it pre-supposes that labor has no interest in price stability or that its leaders see no relation between wage increases (in excess of productivity) and price increase. This may well, within limits, be true, but the limits I predict will prove to be very important. Moreover, the loose yielding to wage increases by corporations could be greatly reduced by legislation designed to prevent price increases within six months after the collective bargain went into effect, unless, in the meantime, a Board of Inquiry had ruled the price increases justifiable.[3] Today there is much greater concern about these matters than in the days of the gold standard when prices rose (1896–1914) 2½ per cent, compound rate, *per annum*. I am optimistic enough to believe that here as elsewhere we shall find our way.

"Deficit financing," while appropriate to reduce cyclical unemployment, must not become so ambitious, warns Fellner, as to create chronic inflationary pressure. And it *cannot* be "used successfully to prevent minor fluctuations in employment (minor recessions) without sacrificing other essential objectives," such as freedom from direct controls. The policy can only be applied "when contraction has spread over the economy as a whole," and to stop a *"cumulative downward tendency toward a condition of mass unemployment."*

I am compelled to say that I find this statement rather shocking. Here Fellner appears to revert to the thinking prior to the Great Depression. Then it was often argued that action should not be taken, if at all, until late in the depression when things were really getting serious. This seems, indeed, to be what Fellner is saying.

So much for purely cyclical policy. But if a significant

[3] This suggestion is a kind of hybrid between one made by myself several years ago and one made recently by Professor Galbraith in the *Atlantic Monthly*, January 1957.

deficiency of private investment in relation to full employment savings were to become chronic, and the deficiency were made up by the government, the result, Fellner thinks, would be thoroughgoing institutional change. Such a policy, he believes, would spell the end of the private enterprise system.

Now what are the grounds for this conclusion? Two types of arguments can be and are employed. For one thing, it can be argued that the requisite budget would have to be so large that if tax-financed two disastrous consequences would necessarily follow: (a) the tax system would destroy the private enterprise system, and (b) it would heavily assume the form of public investment in areas that compete with private enterprise. The result would be to further reduce private investment or even completely suppress it. True this last difficulty, says the author, could be avoided by undertaking large-scale transfer payments or subsidies to consumers in place of public investment outlays. But this, he argues, would routinize economic activities and render the system so static as not to require any private initiative. The entrepreneurial function would have lost its substance.

These sweeping conclusions are, I believe it is fair to say, entirely *obiter dicta*—personal opinions of the author (no doubt shared by many who are skeptical of modern developments). They are set forth, as so often in the history of economic doctrines, as self-evident truths. But is it really true that experience (and we have quite a little by now) and common observation support these conclusions? Are they plausible in view of general knowledge of the course of events?

Fellner believes it to be self-evident that the current tax system weighs so heavily on business that the large tax-financed budget of recent years has had no expansionary effect in the economy. While he believes in principle that the balanced budget is expansionist (the balanced-budget theorem), he doubts that it in fact has been in the postwar years. Anyone is, of course, free to believe that, but informed opinion would, I believe, support the contention that *experience* contradicts this view. Experience discloses, despite the high corporate taxes, not only a boom level of investment but a level that has been sustained without serious interruption for a longer period than ever before in our history.[4] Experience demonstrates that profits after taxes have been beyond the dreams of even the most optimistic. The stock market has nodded its approval, and business confidence has registered itself in a volume of investment which has raised our capacity to turn out basic materials 60 per cent in nine years. Moreover, the able researches on the effect of taxes on incentives by economists in the Harvard School of Business Administration provide empirical evidence which runs directly counter to the view here expressed. Finally, a reading of the financial press in the last few years overwhelmingly indicates that general informed opinion regards the large tax-financed budget as strongly expansionist.

This leads us to the next step. Assume that this be granted, is not this favorable result due to the fact that the budget is largely military—an area non-competitive with private enterprise. A budget of similar size composed of peacetime outlays could have a quite different effect on private enterprise.

Here we are clearly on more debatable ground, yet, on balance, I believe that experience and available empirical data are sufficient to challenge this view. The problem involves partly the size of a peacetime budget, and partly the character of the expenditures.

First, with respect to size. It is indeed a fact that the budget must be fairly large in order to make the compensatory devices

---

[4] In the ten years 1947–56, the ratio of gross private fixed-capital investment to GNP topped that of the boom year 1929.

(tax adjustments, borrowing from the public or from the banking system) adequately effective. However, the minimum conceivable budget for the United States has by now reached a magnitude (whatever may happen to international relations) amply large, *when properly financed*, to furnish the expansionist effect needed for sustained full employment. There is therefore no need to enlarge the budget *artificially* beyond what is urgently needed on its own merits, account being taken of social and economic priorities. Fiscal policy advocates have never, as far as I know, advocated a wasteful blowing-up of the budget merely to provide jobs.

We come then to the matter of the *character* of the outlays. Will they compete with and supplant private enterprise? At once it is necessary to clear the ground with respect to one point. Any new undertaking, whether public or private, will step on the toes of certain established activities. This is the nature of progress. The question therefore relates to the effect on private enterprise *as a whole,* not the effect on this or that sector alone. The public power developments in the Tennessee Valley and in the Pacific Northwest may perhaps have supplanted private power to a degree, but private enterprise as a whole has been greatly stimulated. Fellner takes far too narrow a view of the proper scope of public resource development—he mentions schools, hospitals, roads, flood regulation. Take flood regulation for example. This is not something that stands apart by itself. It is a part of a big bundle which quickly leads us into controversial issues. When is "public power" competitive, and when is it a project which almost everyone will agree can best be undertaken by the federal government?

Actually on a strictly economic basis, the public power issue, and indeed resource development generally, is currently being debated on far too restricted grounds. The merits of a resource development project can never be measured by the self-liquidating yardstick. It is not enough to ask whether the project will be profitable to the corporation (or government Treasury) undertaking the venture. The proper question is rather: Will it be a profitable undertaking *from the standpoint of the economy as a whole?* The gains in cost-reducing *productivity* for the economy as a whole will almost certainly by far exceed the net revenues of the enterprises undertaking the project. Such developments tend to raise the profitability of industry generally. Only in the event that the developing corporation owned *all* the industries in the area affected could it measure the over-all economic effect of the venture in terms of its own net revenue. For this reason, only the federal government can carry resource development to the point justified by the over-all effect on aggregate industry. Private enterprise cannot go beyond the narrow, self-liquidating criterion. This point has not been fully grasped even by the public power advocates. Public resource development can open up vast private investment opportunities. Such projects resemble technological and innovational developments.[5] And, from the standpoint of growth, public outlays on human resource development may well have even greater expansionist effects than equal outlays on physical capital projects.

At one point Fellner recognizes this argument to a degree. External economies, he says, are said to develop when, by increasing its factor-input, a firm not merely raises its own output but also increases output elsewhere in the economic system. The free market, he says, provides insufficient rewards for activities involving external economies because part of

---

[5] It is useful to distinguish between "high-powered" investment and ordinary investment. Transportation, power developments, and the like, are "high-powered" in the sense that they have a magnified effect on cost reduction and on the productivity of all the industries which depend on the basic industries. In contrast, much factory investment, while indeed satisfying consumer wants (clothes, etc.), add nothing to the productivity of industry in general.

the social benefit of investment is "given away" by the investor. This puts the case very well indeed, and I wholly agree.

Viewing the matter *historically*, Fellner takes a somewhat more liberal position with respect to the role of public investment. He points out that all along in history the profitability of private investment projects has been influenced by governmental undertakings. Governments assisted in the initial accumulation of capital stock—roads, canals, ships, buildings. They provided in considerable measure an incentive for private capital accumulation.

Apart from resource development, the backlog of peacetime budgetary requirements is far greater, I suggest, than Fellner recognizes. On the urgent needs of modern communities—schools, teachers' salaries, community cultural and recreational activities, hospitals, medical research, roads, urban redevelopment, housing, crime and delinquency, etc.—we have by now an immense amount of documentary evidence. None of this is taken account of by Fellner. Accordingly it is not difficult for the author to reach the conclusion that a large peacetime budget would tend to supplant private enterprise. But the evidence contradicts this view.

Let it be noted that the large budget of the welfare state does not mean that the government itself becomes a large producer.[6] It does indeed, directly or indirectly (through transfer payments) become a large purchaser of goods produced by private industry. Thus, despite the enormous growth of the federal budget, the ratio of government employees to private employees in productive enterprises increased only slightly from 1.3 per cent in 1929 to 1.8 per cent in 1950.[7]

The welfare state has by now a fairly considerable history.

[6] On p. 365, Fellner speaks of tax-financed government "output" and tax-financed government "production" as though a large budget means the same thing as government operated productive enterprise.

[7] See *America's Needs and Resources* (Twentieth Century Fund, 1955).

But there is no visible evidence, either here or in western Europe, that the entrepreneurial function has lost or is losing its substance. On the contrary sustained full employment offers unparalleled stimulus to entrepreneurial inventiveness and ingenuity. Give a business man an *adequate market* and you can be fairly sure that he will find his way. Where is the evidence that the welfare state and the unprecedented role of government budgets have resulted or are likely to result in "essentially routinized economic activities," which require no private initiative? Private enterprise has been and is proving itself to be a pretty tough animal—an animal which thrives very well indeed on an adequate food supply, namely adequate aggregate demand.

Throughout most of the volume, Fellner assumes that healthy growth demands not only a *small* government budget but also a *balanced* budget. He allows short-period deficits for his limited cyclical compensatory program. Later he goes a little further. Over the long run, to offset a *minor chronic* insufficiency of private investment, budget deficits may, to a small degree, be allowed to overbalance periods of budget surpluses. "What is important here is not the arbitrary concept of long-run 'budgetary balance,' or prevention of the rise in the public debt. What matters is our ability to maintain appreciable and strong growth rates with primary reliance on private investment activity."

With this latter statement I heartily concur. What I find missing, however, is an examination of the role of liquid assets (government securities and deposits) in the modern economy. If our GNP can double in 20 to 25 years, would not such growth be facilitated by a more or less corresponding increase in liquid monetary assets? The role of growth in the holdings of U.S. securities by banks, by savings institutions, and by corporations in a growing economy deserves, I feel, extended analysis in a volume which stresses the importance for economic growth of a flexible and elastic monetary system. It is not enough simply to say that a "growing economy with a growing national income, and thus a growing tax base, can stand a gradually increasing public debt." What is needed is an analysis of the role of the public debt as an instrument of public policy designed to promote growth and expansion. It is, however, fair to add that Fellner firmly asserts that "precise balancing of the budget, in the short run or in the long run, is not a meaningful objective." The dangers, he adds, of a "rule of thumb, such as that of precise budgetary balance, are extremely grave." We are compelled to "place our trust in discretionary policies to prevent major cyclical depressions and mass unemployment." The gradual recognition of this truth, he feels, "by fundamentally conservative groups is a political fact of great importance." [8]

Fellner fears not only that the large budget of the welfare state is likely irretrievably to damage the private enterprise system, but also that the "equality-security characteristics or other environmental properties of our time" may themselves produce stagnation tendencies.

From this and many other passages scattered throughout the volume, it becomes clear that he is highly skeptical of the mixed public-private economy of today. Far from holding, as I do, that the mixed economy has greatly strengthened capitalism, he views (as did Schumpeter) this whole development as a dead weight on the economy. Arterial sclerosis is creeping into the system or at least there is, one gathers, a danger of this. A little of the welfare-state drug, perhaps even the dose already taken, is tolerable, but not much more. He accepts a limited use of compensatory fiscal policy, and is reasonably optimistic that we can carry the burden of the institutional changes thus far introduced. "The influence of

[8] Recently, however, Secretary Humphrey has bluntly disclosed that influential conservative thinking is still far behind Professor Fellner.

these equality-minded and security-minded groups has lifted the proposition that mass unemployment is intolerable from the status of a subjective value judgment to that of a statement of fact." And this creates for him a problem. Still he does not advocate a rooting out of trade unionism or even a weakening of the welfare state thus far reached. While deploring these tendencies, he still finds it "difficult to believe that these various direct effects of unionism should decisively interfere with the long-run tendency toward satisfying the growth corollaries." High graduated taxation and the pressure toward redistribution springs in large part, he says, from organized labor. This could weaken the performance of industrial nations. However, it is not feasible, he thinks, to make categoric statements about precise limits of tolerance or the point at which these tendencies become "truly threatening." Quantitative appraisals cannot be undertaken with scientific accuracy.[9]

Fellner fails altogether to reconcile his attitude toward redistribution of income with his acceptance of the view that in advanced countries the propensity to save may be too high. It would, however, be consistent with his views to inquire what is the *optimum* degree of equality of income distribution. In economics it is always the *optimum* point that is important, and this changes with changing circumstances. As everyone knows, every economic policy can be carried too far. It is, however, quite indefensible to assume that this fact *per se* constitutes a valid argument against advances in social policy. This kind of discussion leaves us in the mire. It provides no solid footing. We are told that "if the equalitarian creed

---

[9] This caution is well placed. But statements like the following, while self-evident, are scarcely very helpful. Here is a sample: "That it is feasible to increase tax graduation to a point where it would put an end to the longrun tendency toward satisfying the growth corollaries in the private-enterprise framework is beyond doubt" (p. 378).

displaces the outlook of the market economy," the growth process will cease. But this scarcely provides a guide as to what constitutes "workable blends of the ideology of the market-economy with that of equalitarianism." [10]

The plain statistical fact is that the tendency toward equalitarian distribution has made rather meager progress thus far, and it may well be that it has not been carried nearly far enough in terms of a workable capitalism which requires an appropriate balance between consumption and investment. The wide-spread approval (which I judge Fellner does not share) of the recent findings of the National Bureau of Economic Research indicating a modest shift in the equalitarian direction during the last two decades would seem to indicate the trend of dominant thinking (including that of a fair proportion of business leaders) on this highly important subject.

One final comment. Starting from the condition of stagnation in the interwar period in Europe and in the thirties in the United States, we have fully emerged on to a path of unparalleled growth and expansion. In this development, technology has certainly played a highly important role; and so also an adequate money supply, and to a more limited degree mobility of resources. But a comprehensive appraisal can not overlook the plain fact that a quite *new* factor is the prodigious increase in the fiscal operations of government. Now this is precisely the Keynesian remedy for the stagnation from which we have emerged. It is, moreover, plausible to argue that the resulting condition of adequate aggregate demand has itself been a powerful factor stimulating technological development. Prosperity has enabled corporations to set aside vast sums for technical research, and a pressing market promotes long-range investment planning. In addition,

[10] Elsewhere (pp. 345-46) he suggests that: "Considering the materialistic traits of the market economy, we should not regret that it has come to rule with impurities, that is with softening admixtures."

the adequate (perhaps more than adequate) money supply is clearly related to the budgetary operations of the last 20 years. It requires, it would seem, a pretty heavy black-out of a vast laboratory experiment to believe that this vastly enlarged role of government has really played no role in the spectacular transition from stagnation to sustained growth and expansion. It is not only the high level of activity that is impressive; it is the fact that it has been *sustained for so long a period*, a period exceeding by a considerable margin any past experience.

APPENDIX C

THE PUBLIC DEBT RECONSIDERED

The pros and cons of the public debt will, I have no doubt, be considered by most economists as so thread-bare a topic that it is not worth writing about. Still when so distinguished an economist as the present occupant of the chair once held by Alfred Marshall writes a full-dress article about the adverse effects of a domestic national debt and concludes that it is a "serious and real economic burden" some further discussion may perhaps not be unwarranted.

I

Professor Meade[1] begins his article with a reference to the view that apart from a redistribution of wealth and income a domestic national debt can have little effect on the economy. It is the purpose of the article, he says, to refute this argument.

Professor Meade makes reference to only two articles in a considerable literature—one by Lerner in *Income, Employment and Public Policy* (New York, 1948) and the other by Domar in the *American Economic Review*, xxxiv (December

[1] J. E. Meade, "Is the National Debt a Burden?" *Oxford Economic Papers*, n. s. x (June 1958); and James M. Buchanan, *Public Principles of Public Debt* (Homewood, Illinois, 1958).

1944). But these articles, he says, "show only that debt is unlikely to grow without limit relatively to the national income. They do not show that a given debt has no adverse effects."

The reference to Lerner, in particular, seems to have been rather a casual one, since Professor Meade apparently had not taken time to re-read it. For, in fact, most of the adverse effects elaborated by Meade had already been brilliantly and concisely discussed by Lerner in the article cited.

Meade's major adverse effects of a large national debt may perhaps for convenience be listed as follows: (1) the "Pigou-effect" on saving; (2) the "Kaldor-effect" on incentives to work, invest, and accumulate; (3) the adverse incentive effect of the additional taxes needed to finance interest payments, and particularly the widened gap between the value of the marginal product and the net reward for labor (or investment) caused by high marginal tax rates; (4) the adverse effect of the higher interest rates needed to counter the inflationary impact of the "Pigou-effect."

Before embarking upon a critique of his article, let me quote a few sentences from the Lerner article mentioned above. These quotations will provide the double advantage of setting before us the essence of the adverse effects, and also of showing that the earlier literature, designed to minimize fears of the public debt, did not in fact neglect consideration of adverse effects, including incentive effects. The page references are to Lerner's chapter in *Income, Employment and Public Policy*.

1. "There are also effects on investment. Additional taxes reduce the net yield from investment, after taxes, and make socially useful investments unprofitable to the investor." This effect may be minimized, however, by "balancing losses and profits for tax purposes." Nevertheless the "opportunity of loss offset is not universal, so that the interest payments on

the national debt, by making taxation necessary for the prevention of inflation, interferes with the efficiency of the economy by discouraging useful investments" (page 261).

2. "An increase in the national debt . . . can make the owners of the government bonds less willing to work. One of the reasons for working, the earning of money to put away for a rainy day, is weakened . . . because there is more put away already for rainy days" (page 262, Meade's so-called "Kaldor-effect").

3. "Of real importance is the consideration that taxes necessary to offset the inflationary effects of the interest payments may reduce the net reward for work below the value of the marginal net product. This would reduce the amount of work done below the optimum, and constitute a real impairment of the efficiency of the economy" (page 262). This argument is made much of by Meade. Lerner after dramatizing the point by imagining a fantastically large debt concludes that "this shows that too large a national debt can be a most serious matter" (page 264). And further, "the problem cannot be dismissed by simply recommending good taxes instead of bad taxes," since it is probably impossible to avoid altogether taxes which "fall heavily on the reward for marginal effort" (page 267).

4. "The growth of national debt is an increase in the holdings of wealth . . . and so it relieves the pressure to save" (page 265). This is the "wealth-effect" as Lerner has it, or the so-called "Pigou-effect" as Meade has it. Meade refers to it as the first and foremost effect, but a strangely neglected effect.[2]

[2] Actually the "Pigou-effect," as used by Pigou himself, comes into play as a result of a deflation of prices, not as a result of an *increase* in wealth holdings due to public borrowing or currency creation. What Meade really has in mind is in fact the "wealth-effect," not the "Pigou-effect." While from a purely static standpoint the two come to the same thing, from a dynamic standpoint they are very different. It is therefore doubtful whether it is really appropriate to refer to the

Lerner summarized as follows: The "diminishing desire to work, accompanied by the increasing desire to spend (which accompanies the growth of individual wealth in the form of ownership of national debt) will decrease the supply of goods in the market—even while it increases the demand for them" (page 267).[3]

Meade (in addition to the points which had earlier been made by Lerner as indicated above) has also elaborated arguments which may perhaps be summed up briefly as follows:

1. Even though the tax burden of a large debt may be deliberately kept light by maintaining a low rate of interest, still (despite the fact that in these circumstances tax rates could be cut only a *little* in the event of debt removal) considerable improvement in incentives to save and invest would follow from the fact that the rich wealth holders would (after the debt had been reduced) find themselves in a much lower marginal tax bracket.

2. A large debt, if it should lead to a deliberate policy of keeping the rate of interest low, weakens the effectiveness of monetary policy[4] and so compels greater resort to high tax rates.

3. There is a favorable (or unfavorable) effect of debt removal on the relative prices of bills, bonds, and equities; and

---

"wealth-effect" (springing from *increased* holdings of public debt obligations) as the "Pigou-effect."

Actually the "Pigou-effect," properly speaking, was first stated by Haberler in Chapter 10 of the first edition (1937) of his *Prosperity and Depression*, and reproduced on page 403 in the second and later editions. Thus the "Pigou-effect" proper should perhaps be called the "Haberler-effect" and the "wealth-effect" the "Lerner-effect."

[3] It should be noted that the same incentive effects would follow from an increased accumulation of private asset holdings.

[4] On the contrary, it should be noted, R. V. Roosa, of the New York Federal Reserve Bank, has argued that a large debt makes monetary policy more effective. See my discussion of this matter in my *The American Economy* (New York, 1957), 55–57.

these changes have an impact on inflationary or deflationary pressures. (This is a peculiarly obscure and on the whole inconclusive section.)

4. The effect of debt removal on the money supply could result, he says, in a "catastrophic monetary deflation." Some alternative method would have to be found to control the supply of money. This, he asserts, is the *"sine qua non* for the removal of deadweight debt." [5]

Throughout most of his article, Meade compares a nation before and after debt removal. This removal is accomplished by an "imaginary capital levy" which, it is assumed, leaves everything else unchanged. We may call this the "magic wand" method of debt removal. At the end of his article, however, he finally disposes of the magic wand and considers practical means of reducing the debt. But he is unprepared to say whether the "immediate costs and the ultimate gains of different methods of debt reduction" would justify such action. More about this later.

II

My first criticism relates to Professor Meade's failure to consider the cyclical aspects of his incentive effects. A large

[5] It should be noted that Meade appears to be concerned in fact only with so-called "deadweight debt," which means debt not covered by tangible assets. The implication is that debt created to finance investment in tangible assets is productive, while debt not so invested is unproductive. But this distinction is not tenable. Consider for example debt created to finance scientific research, or for scholarships to help educate scientists, or indeed for education in general. In the United States it is generally believed that the low level of education in the South is perhaps the primary reason for low per capita incomes in that section. And consider the immense amount of tangible assets held by the United States government in the form of military equipment.

national debt can have an important effect on the stability of the economy over the cycle. The "built-in" stabilizer aspect of the wealth-effect (Meade's so-called Pigou-effect) is not even discussed. I regard this aspect of public debt as highly important.

I do not believe that anyone could seriously question the fact that the impact of the wealth effect (its tendency to raise consumer spending) is of far greater moment in depression or recession periods than in boom years. When people hold assets, they can and will spend more freely in periods of unemployment. When, however, they are fully employed at good wages, any *additional* urge to spend by reason of their ownership of assets is not so easy to appraise. Indeed it could be argued, and unquestionably is true in many cases, that the accumulation of a nest egg of savings whets the appetite for more.[6] The plain fact is that we don't know very much about the wealth-effect in highly prosperous periods. In periods of unemployment there can be no question that asset holdings, widely distributed, tend to tilt the slope of the consumption function so as to increase consumption.

If this be true (as I believe it must be) then the public debt, through the "wealth-effect," becomes a powerful built-in stabilizer. Thus I agree with Meade, that the wealth-effect of a public debt is of the first importance, but I reach a different conclusion. Offsetting the adverse effects of the added taxes which must be paid to restrain the income-effect of the public debt is the benefit which all members of the community enjoy from the fact that the debt acts as a built-in stabilizer. The added taxes may be a small price to pay for the added stability. The national debt becomes a

[6] In the United States it was formerly asserted by armchair philosophers that widespread old age security would reduce the role of private life insurance companies. History has proven that quite the opposite in the case.

kind of national insurance system[7] to which we all contribute
as tax payers, and from which we all receive the benefit of
insurance against instability—in short, relative freedom from
any serious decline in consumption expenditures in periods
of recession. A new business just beginning operations will
not like the added taxes; but it will appreciate the added
security to its sales volume.

Quite apart from the wealth-effect as a stabilizer of consumption is another stabilizing aspect of the public debt.
Exactly as in the case of the old-age social security system,
the interest payments continue even in depression, while the
tax liabilities (under a progressive tax structure) decline. This
again helps to maintain consumer demand in recession. And
since the tax revenues (from the rates set to cover interest
payments) rise faster than national income in boom years, this
acts to restrain inflationary pressures. Again, the national debt
serves as a built-in stabilizer.

But now what about the over-all, long-run impact (involving the whole business cycle) of the wealth-effect? Is
there persuasive evidence that a large national debt does indeed
tend to reduce the ratio of saving to disposable income? The
United States—surely the country with the widest distribution of asset holdings incident to a large national debt—may
perhaps serve as a laboratory guinea-pig. Do Americans spend
a larger proportion of their disposable income than they did
in 1929 when the debt was very small? The statistics (*President's Economic Report*, 1958, 130) show the contrary. In
1929 5.0 per cent was saved; 1950–57, an *average* of 7.0 per
cent was saved, with no year falling below 5.8 per cent. Of
course nothing can be *proved* in economics. There are far too
many variables. But it is at any rate quite clear that Meade's

[7] See my *Economic Policy and Full Employment* (New York, 1947),
275, where I discuss the public debt as a kind of national insurance
system.

Pigou-effect does not appear to be a matter for really "serious" concern.

Similarly, the quantitative impact of the tax-effect of the debt does not appear alarming. In 1958 the federal interest charges were indeed 7.6 per cent of the aggregate taxes, Federal, State, and local. While this is not an inconsiderable amount, it is doubtful that a 7 or 8 per cent reduction in taxes would have any startling effect on incentives. Particularly is this the case when it is remembered that the debt also has an income effect—the added money income received by bond holders. When we consider the large holding of government securities by the banking system, the social security trust funds, the life insurance companies, the savings banks, local government, and private pension funds, and the masses of people holding baby bonds—this item becomes one of no negligible importance.

Consider also the marginal-work effect discussed both by Lerner and Meade. What do we really know about it? We know that by and large a man either has a job or he hasn't. It is not a question of small marginal increments. And if he has a job, the pace is set by the factory production system. The employment figures do not indicate that in the United Kingdom and the United States a large public debt prevents people from taking and holding jobs. And the productivity figures do not indicate a slackening of work effort. With respect to *extra* jobs over and above the regular job, high tax rates may indeed *induce* such effort, as in the case of a colleague who announced that the income tax had made such inroads on his disposable income that he was compelled to accept a summer teaching job. In the United States, in high employment periods, hundreds of thousands held down two jobs to a degree quite unprecedented in our history.

I will not bore the reader by citing statistics that are well known. Suffice it to say that for the thirteen year period from 1945 to 1957 inclusive, the *average* ratio of private investment to GNP was equal to or greater than that of any previous *boom* year in our history. Indeed we outdid ourselves in 1955–1957 when investment in plant and equipment increased nearly 40 per cent from an already near-peak level. This burst of investment played a major role in the inflationary pressures of these two years. There appears to be considerable evidence that we have developed over-capacity on a considerable scale in many lines: there is little if any evidence that the incentive to invest has been blunted by the existence of a large national debt.

At this point I may perhaps be permitted a small digression. Meade's incentive analysis (disregarding for the moment the *weight* that may appropriately be assigned to it) has to a degree a certain validity. Indeed it is not infrequently the *only* valid point remaining of popular arguments alleging serious adverse effects of a national debt. One such argument[8] which has had (and still has) an immense vogue is this: Does not the existence of a large public debt tend to prevent desirable and much needed social welfare expenditures? The heavy interest charges, it is alleged, usurp the field. Useful expenditures that could otherwise be made cannot be made. If the national debt were somehow lifted, runs the argument, the money now spent on interest payments could be spent on social welfare projects without imposing any further taxes.

But this argument covers up confusions. Certain important facts must be kept firmly in mind. Interest payments constitute a part of the community's income, and if the debt were removed this part of the aggregate income would disappear. Let us assume that the interest receivers had formerly invested the money in new homes. The debt being lifted, the

[8] Professor Meade does *not* advance the argument here criticized, but the relevance of this discussion to his paper will, I believe, become evident from what follows in the text.

interest payments cease. The tax money (formerly flowing to the interest-receivers) is now employed to purchase public housing. The debt-lifting has therefore not had any effect on the draft on productive resources. The same amount of productive resources is being employed as before in the production of homes. The aggregate amount of goods and services produced remains unchanged. Public housing has been substituted for private housing. The debt-lifting reduced private income and private spending. Taxes remain the same. Tax money is diverted from interest payments to public housing. A shift has occurred in the direction of spending because the debt-lifting has redistributed income.

Much the same result could have been accomplished without the imaginary debt removal. Through debt removal (but no tax reduction) private income was cut down. It could equally well have been cut down by an *increase* in taxes— this *new* tax money being used to buy public housing.

Either way there has occurred a redistribution of income and of spending—more public spending, less private spending.[9] The debt-lifting method hurts because it cuts down private income (taxes are not cut) and also private wealth holdings. The additional tax method hurts because disposable income is cut down though wealth holdings remain unchanged.

Now the point I wish to make has a bearing on Meade's argument. The removal of debt (with no tax cut) does *not*, as is so often alleged, make possible the substitution of useful spending for less useful spending, leaving everything else (including private income) unchanged. What has happened is a reduction of disposable income together with reduction of

[9] In the event that the tax money were used (after the debt had been lifted) to increase social security payments, the net effect would be a redistribution of income and a shift in *private* spending. One transfer payment would have been converted into transfer payments going to another social group with consequent shifts in private spending.

private wealth holdings and also a redistribution of income and of the direction of spending.

The net conclusion then is that the existence of a national debt does not prevent useful public spending. Rather the net effect of lifting the debt has to be assessed on Meade's terms, i.e., the Pigou-effect, the Kaldor-effect, and other incentive effects. My own assessment of these effects, as we have seen, is however different from Meade's.

I have cited the favorable built-in stabilizer effect of a national debt. And there are other favorable effects that are not mentioned by Meade, while others are, I feel, inadequately appraised. A point of great importance is the well-known fact that when national debt increases, private debt tends to remain relatively stationary or even at times to fall. It appears to be a fact, for reasons that are by no means altogether obscure, that the ratio of aggregate debt (public and private) to GNP changes very little.

In the United States aggregate debt constituted 183 per cent of GNP in 1929, 189 per cent in 1940, 190 per cent in 1946, and 173 per cent in 1959. Federal debt increased by $28.3 billion from 1929 to 1940, while private debt[10] *decreased* by $29.3 billion. From 1940 to 1946 federal debt increased by $184.9 billion while private debt remained nearly stationary (increased by only $22.6 billion). From 1946 to 1959, federal debt increased by $13.3 billion while private debt increased by $416.9 billion.[11] The figures relate to *net* federal debt.

[10] I have included state and local government debt with private debt. Not armed with the powers of money creation and almost unlimited powers of taxation over the *whole* economy, state and local governments are much more in the same relatively weak position as private debtors.

If one excluded state and local government debt, however, the difference would not be great. These debts were only $13.2 billion, in 1929, $16.5 billion in 1940, $13.6 billion in 1946, and $55.6 billion in 1959.

[11] *Economic Report of the President* (1958), 170.

Which represents the greater burden on the economy as a whole—the interest charges on private debt, or the tax paid to cover interest charges on the public debt? The answer is certainly not an easy one. It depends upon a great many factors. But one thing is clear: in a depression the tax liabilities decline sharply and this eases the burden in this difficult period. But interest charges on private debt remain fixed. Again it is the built-in stabilizer feature that comes to the fore.

Meade discusses the relation of national debt to the money supply. He admits that if the debt were sharply reduced, new monetary devices would have to be invented. To elaborate this would require another article, and he does not attempt it. Modern nations have by now had long experience in developing far more efficient monetary systems than ever before, largely on the basis of national debt. Why abandon this now? Using the "deadweight" debt criterion it might be said that its removal would still leave enough debt for monetary purposes. This I seriously question. There are good reasons for believing that a country like the United States with a GNP of $500 billion could not function as effectively as it in fact now does without something like the high degree of liquidity which we now enjoy. As the GNP rises over the long run, restrictive tendencies could well develop by reason of an inadequate volume of liquid assets if in fact the debt were not permitted to rise. And matters would be still worse if we undertook drastic debt reduction.

III

Now I should like to comment on the methodology employed by Meade in his analysis.[12] He begins by assuming

[12] On this matter of methodology, Buchanan has some good things to say. But see my criticism later in this article.

two societies similar in every respect except that "history has left" one society with a debt and the other without a national debt. This procedure for any meaningful analysis is not admissible. The countries being similar in every other respect must both have had to face similar situations—wars for example. One chose to finance it by borrowing and the other by taxation. Will that leave them exactly similar later except for the debt? Certainly not. The method chosen to finance the war will profoundly have affected the functioning of the economy both during the war and after. The efficiency of the economy and the stock of real capital assets are likely to be very different in the two cases. The degree to which full employment has been reached both during the war and after is likely to be very different. One cannot assume away such a vast difference in the use of the fiscal powers of the state.

Lerner criticized this type of methodology very effectively in the article cited above: "It is pointed out for example that it is better for an economy to have a smaller rather than a large national debt because the 'wealth-effect' and the 'income-effect' of a larger national debt cause more spending so that more taxes are necessary to prevent inflation. Since the taxes are not ideal taxes, they will to some extent fall on the marginal pay for effort, and they will also discourage useful investment and useful government spending. The national debt thus has a bad effect."

"But is this remark of any use as a guide for policy? Hardly at all. For it is surely not intended to suggest that the debt or a part of it should be repudiated . . . Nor can it be intended to suggest that the borrowing should not have taken place in the past if the borrowing was considered less harmful than the alternative deflationary instruments of taxation or government economies at the time." (Pages 271–72.)

Perhaps Meade himself sensed the impropriety of this method. At any rate he abandoned the notion of two societies with different "histories," and instead resorted to the mysticism of an imaginary capital levy to remove the debt in a *given* society—such removal being accomplished by some magic so that "everything else remained the same." The mysticism of this sleight-of-hand performance becomes clearly visible in the fact that Meade always backs away from any suggestion that his "imaginary" capital levy should in fact be imposed.

The method employed represents a purely static type of analysis. It leaves out of account the impact of the *process of debt creation* upon the economy. But this process may well have had an enormous impact upon the economy's growth and expansion. It is one thing to attempt to assess the adverse and beneficial effects of an already existing debt. It is quite another thing to assess the relative advantages and disadvantages of loan financing versus tax financing. Responsible governments do not create debt just for fun. The origin of the debt and the impact of its creation upon the economy must be considered, not merely the fact that the debt *exists*. Similarly the desirability of debt retirement cannot be determined by the magic-wand method, which unfortunately is not available to humans, but only by assessing the impact upon the economy of various feasible methods of debt retirement. In short a dynamic analysis is required.

Meade finally does consider practical policy questions and concludes that there are three ways to get rid of the debt: (1) by inflation, (2) by continued accumulation of savings out of a rising real income, and (3) by extra taxes, the revenues from which would be applied purely for the sake of debt reduction. And for this purpose he suggests: (a) an annual levy on property and (b) an expenditure tax. These he says interfere little if at all with incentives.

About the first two methods little needs to be said. The first factor has already removed in the last 12 years well over a third of the United States debt burden, so-called. When the second factor is included we find that the debt has by now been reduced to half, in relation to GNP. About the third method, it is difficult to refrain from remarking that if indeed "good" taxes—taxes that do not blunt incentives—are so easily available, then at least one of Meade's major worries about the debt disappears. But economists generally will not, I suspect, easily be persuaded that these taxes are in fact quite that good.

Thus Meade argues that *in addition to* the now generally accepted principles of fiscal policy which approve of budget surpluses, (1) to reduce inflationary pressures, and (2) under certain circumstances, to provide public savings in the interest of capital development and economic growth, he would like "to restore a third old-fashioned argument for a budget surplus," namely to "help reduce the national debt." (Incidentally, the third basis for policy decisions appears to limit the free use of the first two.) And how does he justify this really startling conclusion? On the ground that this action will improve "economic incentives in the future."

A basic question is raised by Meade's "third old-fashioned" argument. Shall *abstract* considerations that are presumed to stand for all time, but about which in fact we know very little, be admitted as *one* determinant of fiscal policy decisions? Or shall this decision be based on dynamic considerations—in short the principles of modern fiscal policy.

Indeed in several sections of his article, Professor Meade does view the problem from a dynamic standpoint. And when this is done the vast complexity of good and bad features of a national debt appear. In these sections Professor Meade is far from being complacent or dogmatic about his conclusions. He describes conditions under which the "consequential improvement in incentives to be expected from a redemption of debt will be very small." He argues that in a cold war situation we cannot say for certain what conclusion the marginal reward analysis will lead to. He suggests circumstances "in a mature economy with a tendency to secular stagnation" in which the disappearance of debt "will have made a deflationary situation still more deflationary." He points out that if the general level of prices is rapidly changing, the "disappearance of the national debt is likely to exert a deflationary influence on the price of equities." And again he suggests that the removal of debt would so affect the supply of money and the level of expected earnings on equities that the effect might be to exert "a strong deflationary force."

We may perhaps sum up his own broad conclusion (page 178) as follows: Because of the Pigou-effect, removal of the debt would cause a cut in consumption and would be deflationary. Entrepreneurs, moreover, would find it harder to finance investment, by reason of diminished liquidity, and this would be deflationary. The effect of such removal on the prices of bills, bonds, and equities would on balance tend to be deflationary. One aspect of the Kaldor-effect—the desire to rebuild private fortunes after debt removal—would tend to stimulate business men to greater enterprise and would increase investment. This would have an expansionist effect. Altogether he concludes as follows: "On balance it would appear probable that, even apart from any effects on the supply of money through the banking system, the disappearance of the deadweight debt would exert a significant deflationary influence." But this, he believes, must be counted in present-day circumstances a great advantage, assuming, however, that the government, despite these strongly deflationary influences, is fully able through monetary and fiscal policy to maintain adequate yet stable demand.

This is of course a very large order, especially since the process of debt reduction itself severely restricts the field for monetary and fiscal action. But if it could be achieved, and if we could assume that highly buoyant conditions will continue to prevail, then Meade is of course right that an easing of inflationary pressures through debt removal would tend in the right direction and might thus provide the "occasion for an otherwise desirable relaxation of monetary and fiscal conditions." But the question still remains: Is this the best way to deal with the inflation problem?

The point that I wish to make here, however, is that on Meade's own terms it is quite clear that the removal of a large part of the debt involves revolutionary changes, the consequences of which (even though the magic wand could be employed) it is by no means easy to assess. And once the magic wand is discarded, Meade himself frankly admits that he does not know how the balance sheet stands. All he is certain of is that economic incentives in certain respects will be improved once we have reached a new sea of calm. But, as we have seen, such limited empirical evidence as we have casts doubt on the potency of the alleged adverse incentive effects. On balance we know very little about it. Experience does not seem to make it a matter of "serious" concern. Indeed this problem fades into oblivion when compared with the gigantic misuse of resources which one currently observes in the American economy, caused basically by the wants and values created by irresponsible advertising—a potent system of mechanized education.[18]

IV

About Buchanan's book on *Public Principles of Public Debt* I shall confine myself to brief comments. Buchanan has some good things to say about methodology with which I in general agree. He would, I believe, agree with my criticism

[18] Cf. my "Standards and Values in a Rich Society," *The American Economy*, 1957; J. K. Galbraith, *The Affluent Society* (Boston, 1958).

of Meade's methodology, and much of what he says along this line about the literature on the public debt is, I feel, valid. In other respects, however, I am unable to see that he has made out a good case.

He argues (against the "new orthodoxy") that the primary real burden of a public debt is shifted to future generations, that public and private debt are fundamentally similar, and that external and internal debt are fundamentally alike.

I cannot help feeling that no inconsiderable part of the disagreement on these issues springs from the fact that the contestants are talking about different things. Were this not the case it is not probable that competent economists could battle over these relatively simple issues over a period of 200 years or so, without coming to definite conclusions. It is always possible to make rigid definitions and assumptions and to rule out of the discussion matters that in fact are highly relevant.

Thus, for example, Buchanan says that public and private debt are basically alike. Yet an unbridgeable difference exists in the fact that the national government has the power (a) to issue money (either directly or through the central bank) and (b) to tax all of its citizens. As a borrower this puts the national government in a class by itself. No private borrower has at his command either of these vast financial resources. This fact alone makes a national debt something very different from a private debt, and on this issue nothing more needs really to be said. But in fact much more can be said. For example, an increase in public debt increases the property holdings of the country—the wealth-effect. Increases in private debt can have no such effect. There are many other matters such as those already discussed by Meade and Lerner. There are, of course, many similarities between public and private debt. This no one denies, and if one concentrates on these alone one can quite easily tell a considerable story.

Or take the matter of external and internal debt. Here again Buchanan makes some sensible remarks. There are nonetheless important respects in which external and internal debt are fundamentally unlike. True, public investments made from the proceeds of an external debt may well add enough to real income to cover, and more than cover, the interest charges. And (when resources are not already fully employed) the same applies to public investments made from the proceeds of an internal debt. But in the former case, the foreign exchange mechanism will demand payment in real terms (unless further loans are made), while in the latter case, the added output is consumed at home or else exchanged for other goods in foreign trade. Moreover in the case of domestic debt, cyclical adverse balance of payments problems are not intensified as they may well be in the case of external debt. And in the event of depression (or recession) consumer income is sustained by internal interest payments, while at the same time under a progressive tax structure, tax payments decline. Thus the internal debt serves as a built-in stabilizer. No such stabilizing effect can emerge from an external debt.

With respect to the matter of shifting the burden to future generations, the issue basically relates to the impact of the borrowing process and the resulting debt upon the real income of the future generation as a whole. If wartime borrowing[14] achieves a smoother shift of resources to the war effort, if it produces fuller and more efficient use of resources, then the society will emerge from the war stronger and better equipped to go forward. If this is the case (and I believe most economists would subscribe to this view) it follows that the future generation will have benefited from moderate wartime

[14] Of course there could be too much borrowing. There is probably an optimum rate of wartime borrowing varying with the intensity of the war and other factors. We may well have exceeded this optimum during World War II.

borrowing. There remains the incentive problem which we have already discussed, and the fact that future tax payers must pay more taxes to offset the inflationary effects of the added money income received by the bondholders. On balance is the future generation better or worse off by reason of the debt? Probably no unequivocal answer can be given to this question, but it is in these terms that the so-called shifting problem must be discussed.

The conventional argument that no shifting occurs simply because the job of producing the war materiel and fighting the battles must be borne by the present generation and can not in the nature of the case be borne by future generations—this argument, while significant and important, does not come to grips with the real issue. All too often, it has been assumed by the "new orthodoxy" that this is all that need be said. On the other hand, Professor Buchanan appears to exclude altogether the matter of real sacrifices—harder work and restricted consumption—and to limit himself too exclusively to financial considerations. It is however the *real* factors that are important: in particular the impact of the borrowing upon the *real* income and *real* assets of future generations.

INDEX

CPSIA information can be obtained
at www.ICGtesting.com
Printed in the USA
BVHW042332241019
562039BV00005B/20/P